Freemasons: Tales From The Craft

Steven L. Harrison, 33°, PM, FMLR

Softworx, Inc. Publishing
United States

Freemasons: Tales From The Craft

Copyright © 2014, Steven L Harrison

All original photos and sketches
Copyright © 2014, Steven L Harrison

ISBN 978-1-312-34448-8

Missouri Lodge of Research Edition

9 8 7 6 5 4 3 2 1

All rights reserved. No part of this book may be reproduced or transmitted in any form or by any means, electronic or mechanical, including photocopying, recording, or by any information storage and retrieval system, without the written permission of the author.

For the memories:
From a hot pepper flame-out to twilight picnics in the park;
From Turtle Creek to Rose Mary to River Bend;
From lofty academic achievements to something called Prevuze;
And because logic is the last refuge and 400 is perfect,
I dedicate this book...

To Carolyn

FOREWORD

"If history was told as stories, more people would know it."

~Brother Rudyard Kipling
Hope and Esperance Lodge 782, India

Freemasonry has been around for a long time, and as I've said in my own books, the Fraternity has always had a knack of attracting industrious men. There are few places you can look in American history, and not find a Freemason (or two or three) right in the middle of whatever historical event you're reading about. You'll find Freemasons in key roles in the Revolutionary War. You'll find them at Gettysburg. You'll find them at the Alamo. They played a key role in our expansion westward. Quite a few were American Presidents. And you'll even find a good number of them have been to space. Freemasons have been great scientists, artists, musicians, actors, politicians, soldiers, explorers, industrialists, athletes, and writers. Freemasons have been policy makers, movers, and shakers for centuries. For Masonic writers like Steven Harrison and myself, finding and telling these stories about Freemasons and the roles they've played in our history is a source of endless fascination and inspiration.

Writing about history is easy. Anyone who has written a history term paper in school knows it isn't hard to find facts and write a paper about just about any historical topic. But writing history that people want to read is very difficult. The author has to take the reader out of the present world, and put them in that moment in history. If it's done well, the reader forgets he's being educated, because he's being entertained. A good history writer never loses track of the most important part of writing — the art of telling the story. Brother Rudyard Kipling had it right — great history writers should be storytellers first. And Steven Harrison is a master storyteller.

Steve and I have been friends for several years — we met and became friends because we have the same interests. We enjoy discovering and writing those stories where history and Freemasonry cross paths, and the challenges of finding just the right way to tell the story so that the reader becomes completely absorbed in the narrative.

One of my favorite books is Steve Harrison's book *Freemasonry Crosses the Mississippi*. It's a book I go back to time and time again. Steve and I have written about some of the same men, and some of the same events in history, but our approach to the stories couldn't be more different. I think I go back to his book so often because Steve really knows how to tell a story. He pulls the reader into the story early, captures the reader's attention, and within that first paragraph the reader forgets he's reading history, and is simply in it for the story.

My copy of his first book *Freemasonry Crosses the Mississippi* is what you might describe as "well-thumbed." Nothing pleased me more than when Steve told me he was working on another book — another collection of great stories. It was a great honor when he asked me to write the introduction for his new book considering he is one of my favorite writers and someone that, through his writing, has taught me a great deal about the art of story telling.

So lean back and prepare to enjoy a few great stories told by a somebody that really knows how to tell them. They're stories about all of us, and where we come from. They are stories about moments in history that mattered, and men who overcame the challenges of their times and left their mark on the world. Some of these men and moments you'll undoubtedly know, and others, you'll be experiencing for the first time. And as you're reading, try and imagine what our world might be like today if it weren't for these moments, and these remarkable men, who just happened to be Freemasons.

Todd E. Creason, 33°
Author of *Famous American Freemasons*

PREFACE

Freemasons have been far more prevalent on the world stage than most people know. They are men and supportive women who have generally had a positive impact on society and history. They have led interesting lives and in some cases have been involved in remarkable, even unbelievable incidents.

In 1947, Most Worshipful Brother William R. Denslow came to the staff of the Royal Arch Mason magazine charged with the responsibility of increasing subscriptions and improving content. Building on the knowledge of some of the captivating things Freemasons had done, he came up with the idea of publishing stories about them in what became one of the most popular parts of the magazine. For several years afterward, the inside back cover of the RAM was a page called "*Did You Know*." There, with professional illustrations, he detailed interesting, quirky, even shocking Masonic facts. He later disclosed Brothers would tell him they could not wait for the next edition of the magazine to see that section.

The Royal Arch Magazine published 68 "*Did You Know*" editions in all. Each was skillfully illustrated either by Arthur Sullard, Past Grand Commander of Missouri, or Livonia Scott Ebbe, a prolific Masonic artist. Then, in 1965, Brother Wes Cook, as a part of the Transactions of the Missouri Lodge of Research for that year, compiled all of Denslow's back page articles, along with other Masonic vignettes into a book with the same title, *Did You Know*.

That book has become the single most popular selection of the Missouri Lodge of Research and is one of the few it has reprinted. It is fascinating reading and its stories have been quoted in other publications and websites around the world; and it served as the starting point of the project that culminated in the publication of this book.

Captivated by the information in *Did You Know*, I realized it contained only a fraction of similar stories about the lives of Freemasons and the events surrounding them. I also realized that

Masonry didn't cease in 1965 when the publication of the vignettes stopped, and many more stories since then needed to be told.

This book contains most of the vignettes published in *Did You Know*. Each has been re-researched, re-written and expanded, if necessary. It also contains hundreds of additional tales of a similar nature.

Each story is, for the most part, separate and independent from the others. I tinkered around with various ways to organize the book into chapters and even thought of presenting the items more or less in chronological order. No matter what I tried, however, I kept coming back to the idea that they are best presented in random order, exactly as they appeared in *Did You Know*.

I might add, this book is for fun. It's not a history book or an academic work. I have verified and found some form of corroboration on every story in it, but I have not gone through the rigorous formal research that would be required by a more serious work. Please enjoy it for what it is.

No author writes in a vacuum. I want to thank everyone who has helped with this effort. They are too many to name individually, but among them are my Brothers at Liberty and Kearney Lodges, the Liberty York Rite Bodies, the St. Joseph Scottish Rite and the Missouri Lodge of Research. Coincidentally, I finished writing this book during my term as Master of the Missouri Lodge of Research, which made it the annual book selection for its members. Thanks to my entire officers' line: Harvey Soule, Senior Warden; Gail Turner, Junior Warden; Ron Miller, Secretary-Treasurer; Scott Houge, Senior Deacon; John Hess, Junior Deacon; Randy Davis, Senior Steward; Ron Jones, Junior Steward; Brent Stewart, Marshall; Dale Roller, Chaplain; and Doug Reece, Tyler.

Thanks to Aaron Shoemaker, the Lodge of Research's Editor. In that capacity he does a masterful job of bringing world-class Masonic speakers to our Truman Lecture Series, and also manages the selection of our books, including this one.

As always, the Grand Lodge officers of the state of Missouri have been very helpful and supportive; a special thanks goes to this year's Grand Master, Jon Broyles, who appointed me to the advancing line of the Lodge of Research.

I am also grateful for the efforts of Illustrious Brother Todd E. Creason for writing the foreword to this book. Todd is a talented and prolific Masonic author who discovered my online Blog, which contained much of the material in this book. He invited me to join the writing group he founded, the *Midnight Freemasons*. Each member of that group, led by Managing Editor Robert Johnson, has also been encouraging and supportive.

Finally, but foremost, thanks to my wife Carolyn who edited this book. She has the unique ability to take the things I write and turn them into something worth reading. Her advice, counsel and support have been priceless.

So, with a tip of the hat to Brothers Denslow, Cook and Sullard, as well as to Livonia Scott Ebbe, read on and have a little fun with a few tales from the craft.

Upon The Level And By The Square

In 1830, Brother James Pain, while overseeing the rebuilding of Baal's Bridge in Limerick, Ireland discovered a brass square dated 1507, and bearing the inscription, "I will strive to live with love & care upon the level by the square." The relic is now located at Ancient Union Lodge 13 at the North Munster Masonic Centre in Limerick.

Ireland's Grand Lodge Building

In Ireland, the Grand Lodge building stands on the property where Richard Parsons, First Earl of Rosse, Ireland's first Grand Master, once lived.

The Financial Genius Who Died Penniless

Haym Salomon, a member of King Solomon Lodge 12 in Pennsylvania, was an American Revolutionary hero. Captured and sentenced to death, he escaped to become a broker who practically single-handedly obtained the funds for the US to fight the revolution. He also gave financial assistance to several influential leaders including Thomas Jefferson, James Madison and Edmund Randolph. He was regarded as a financial genius for his role but, amazingly, he died penniless.

Skyscraper

At 22 stories (302 feet) tall, when it was built in 1892, the Chicago Masonic Temple was the world's tallest structure, with an impressive Lodge room at the very top. It was so dominant a feature on the Chicago skyline, it brought the word "skyscraper" into popular use. From the top visitors claimed they could see Council Bluffs, Iowa. Built to last at least a century, wrecking crews demolished it after only 47 years. Two factors led to its demise. First, built at a time when architects did not know much about the logistics of tall buildings, several  of its rooms at the top served as theaters and places for social gatherings. Unfortunately, the elevators could not handle the large crowds going to those places and the building fell out of favor as a social venue. Then, in 1939, Chicago began building the State Street subway, which ran underneath the building and would have required an expensive retrofitting of its foundation. Given that, and the fact that the social set had long since gone elsewhere, the great Chicago Masonic Temple came down.

Mark Twain Gavel

Returning from the Holy Land in 1868, Brother Samuel Clemens (Mark Twain) presented this gavel, made from a cedar tree near Jerusalem, to Polar Star Lodge. Courtesy Polar Star Rose Hill Lodge 79, St. Louis.

Lindbergh's Artificial Heart

Charles Lindbergh, Keystone Lodge 243, St. Louis, once appeared on the cover of Time Magazine, not for any of his accomplishments in aviation, but for his role in inventing what was called an artificial heart.

The First Tyler In Kansas

The first Tyler at a Masonic Lodge meeting in Kansas was a Native American woman. Lydia Walker (Her tribal name was Mendias) served at the station outside while the Freemasons, including her husband Matthew serving as Senior Deacon, met inside. Her house at 350 Troupe in Kansas City, Kansas, served as the Lodge for that first meeting as well as the first meeting place of the Eastern Star in the state. Ms. Walker eventually became the first Grand Matron of the Kansas Eastern Star.

Democrats, Republicans, Progressives, Dixiecrats

Four candidates emerged in the hard-fought presidential campaign of 1948: Republican Thomas Dewey, Progressive Henry Wallace, Dixiecrat Strom Thurmond and the eventual winner, Democrat Harry Truman. Although the candidates were intense rivals and had very different political views, all four were Freemasons.

Initiated On His 21st Birthday

Ray V. Denslow (1885 - 1960) was a prolific Masonic author and Grand Master of Missouri, 1931 - 1932. Among his best known books are *Territorial Masonry, A Missouri Frontier Lodge, The Masonic Conservators, History of Royal Arch Masonry in Missouri, Freemasonry and the Presidency* and many more. He was the first Grand Master to open the Missouri Grand Lodge outside of the state, when he presided over a meeting at the dedication of the  George Washington National Masonic Memorial. MWB Denslow was a third-generation Mason whose father and grandfather instilled in him a fervency for the Craft that lasted a lifetime. So great was his excitement for Freemasonry that he was initiated at the earliest moment possible on his 21st birthday.

A Single Social Security Check

Brother Harland Sanders, Hugh Harris Lodge 938, Corbin, Kentucky, Started his huge Kentucky Fried Chicken franchise empire with nothing more than a single Social Security Check.

Masonry In Action

Brother Roy Clark, Hall of Fame country singer, once related this story about Masonry in action: "We were on tour in Regina, Saskatchewan. Our guitar player, Frank Sandusky, had a blood vessel suddenly rupture in his neck, was rushed to the hospital, and the doctor's report was grave. When local brethren found out he was a Mason they sent for his wife. They took her in, saw that she got back and forth to the hospital, and saw to her needs. It didn't cost her anything, and made an unpleasant situation more bearable — and that is what Masonry is all about. Frank is with us today, as my 'right arm' in the band... I know of no other organization where you have a friend all over the world. It gives you peace of mind, especially traveling as much as we do."

Not Just A Boy Scout

Daniel Carter "Dan" Beard (1850-1941), was best known as the organizer of the Boy Scout movement in the US. A member of Mariners' Lodge 67, New York City and later Cornucopia Lodge 563, Flushing, NY, Brother Beard was also a prolific author and illustrator. Long before the founding of the Boy Scouts, he became a lifelong friend of Brother Samuel Clemens (a.k.a Mark Twain) and illustrated Twain's book, "A Connecticut Yankee in King Arthur's Court."

From Hungary To The Vintners Hall Of Fame

Agoston Haraszthy, was a Hungarian nobleman who emigrated to the US in 1840 and settled in Wisconsin. A member of Madison Lodge 5, he was the first Hungarian to settle permanently in the United States. He founded the oldest incorporated village in Wisconsin, today known as Sauk City. In 1849, he moved to California where he established the state's renowned wine industry. In March, 2007, the Culinary Institute of America recognized his pioneering efforts by inducting him into the Vintners Hall of Fame.

Disney's Body — The Cold Facts

Urban legends abound that former DeMolay Walt Disney's body was cryogenically frozen in anticipation of reviving him one day. The fact is Disney's body was cremated. His ashes are interred at Forest Lawn Cemetery, Los Angeles.

A Soft Baritone Voice

Nat "King" Cole, a member of Thomas Waller Lodge 49 in Los Angeles, was an American jazz pianist, singer and one of the first African Americans to have his own television show. Since his death in 1965, he has remained enormously popular worldwide, adding five posthumous Grammys to the single one he received during his lifetime. Cole owed his success to a soft baritone voice. He was convinced smoking enhanced his rich singing tone and maintained a three-pack-a-day habit during his adult years. Prior to each recording session, he would smoke several cigarettes in quick succession to enhance the effect. Regrettably, the practice took his life at the young age of 45 when he died of lung cancer in 1965.

Fuel For The Doolittle Raid

On April 18, 1942, James "Jimmy" Doolittle, Hollenbeck Lodge 319, Los Angeles, California, led 16 B-25 medium bombers into Japan completing the first successful attack on the Japanese mainland in World War II. Brother Doolittle's heroism during this mission, today known as the Doolittle Raid, earned him the Congressional Medal of Honor. The mission would not have been possible without the high-octane aviation fuel, which enabled the bombers to fly the long distance from the US fleet to Japan. That same high-octane aviation fuel was developed in the previous decade by none other than Brother Doolittle himself.

Creating An American Icon

Danny Thomas (1912 - 1991), a member of Gothic Lodge 270 in Hamilton Square, New Jersey, was an American night club entertainer, television Star, producer and the founder of the St. Jude Children's Research Hospital. Born Amos Muzyad Yakhoob Kairouz, Brother Thomas was best known for his role in the television show Make Room for Daddy. A devout Roman Catholic, Brother Thomas was also an avid golfer with a handicap of ten, one of the original owners of the Miami Dolphins, the sponsor of two PGA tour tournaments and the first non-Jewish member of Hillcrest country club in Los Angeles.

In a 1960 episode of his TV show, Thomas was inadvertently responsible for creating an American icon. In that episode, a country-bumpkin sheriff stopped Thomas' character for speeding. The plot followed Thomas' trials and tribulations while dealing with the small town sheriff, who was also the town judge and newspaper editor. That popular episode turned out to be a pilot for one of TV's most enduring shows, featuring the exploits of that country sheriff, played by Andy Griffith. Griffith was not a Freemason, but held the Fraternity in high regard and actually got his comedic start playing summers at the Dare County Shrine Club.

Brother Thomas was also a member of the Scottish Rite and Al Malaikah Shrine. He received the Congressional Gold Medal and in 2012, the US Postal Service honored him by issuing a "Forever" stamp recognizing his humanitarian accomplishments.

Black Sam

Samuel Fraunces, Holland Lodge 8 of New York City, owned the Fraunces Tavern in New York and served as George Washington's household steward from 1789-94. Born in the West Indies, Brother Fraunces was called "Black Sam," indicating he was an African American. Portraiture, however shows a light-skinned individual and confuses speculation about his heritage. Researchers have suggested he might have been the son of black and white parents but the fact is, his race remains unknown.

Humberto Moreira

No less than fifteen Presidents of Mexico have been Freemasons: Miguel Aleman, Nicholas Brave, Anastasio Bustamante, Plutarco E. Calles, Lazaro Cardenas, Ignacio Comonfort, Porfirio Diaz, Emilio Portes Gil, Manual Gonzalez, Vincinte Guerrero, Augustin de Iturbide, Benito Juarex, Francisco Madero, Archduek Maximilian and Antonio Lopez de Santa Anna.

Recent presidents of Mexico have not been Masons, but a number of the Grand Lodges and the Scottish Rite there are closely identified with the ruling party "Partido Revolucionario Institucional" (PRI). Humberto Moreira, the leader of that party, and former Governor of the State of Coahuila (2005-2011) is not only a Freemason, but is also the Sovereign Grand Inspector General of the Supreme Council for Mexico. Brother Moreira is considered a potential future president of Mexico. A grandson of Brother Rubén Moreira Cobo (a former SGIG of Mexico), he has worked diligently to unite competing Grand Lodges in his country. Most see his efforts as being successful. He says he sees the unification of the Mexican Lodges as being "important for achieving a platform of peace, unity and fraternal communication."

A Grade School Education

Brothers George Washington, Andrew Jackson and Andrew Johnson each became President of the United States without having anything more than a grade school education.

High Sentiments

President Calvin Coolidge was not a Freemason, but while Governor of Massachusetts he had this to say about the fraternity when he addressed the Grand Lodge there: "It has not been my fortune to know much of Freemasonry, but I have had the great fortune to know many Freemasons, and I have been able in that way to judge the tree by its fruits. I know of your high ideals. I have seen that you hold your meetings in the presence of the open Bible and I know that men who observe that formality have high sentiments of citizenship, of worth and of character. That is the strength of our commonwealth and nation."

Brother Ford And The Giant Chicken

A giant chicken-outfit-clad stalker hounded President Gerald Ford in his 1976 presidential campaign. The huge "Pollo Loco" followed Ford from campaign stop to campaign stop, at times sharing the stage with him, interviewing him and even embracing him. Rather than becoming annoyed, Brother Ford played along with the prank and brought some levity to an otherwise dreary campaign. Today, that same "chicken" who made his national debut campaigning with Gerald Ford has gone on to fame in his own right. He is now known as The San Diego Chicken.

A Small Technicality

Bernard Pierre Magnan (1791-1865) was a French statesman and soldier who supported Napoleon III in his successful coup d'etat of 1851. Magnan's loyalty won the Emperor's enduring support and, in return he appointed Magnan Marshal of France. Then, in 1862, Napoleon had Magnan installed as the Grand Master of the Grand Orient de France (GODF). Many objected to the appointment due to a "small technicality" — at the time of his installation as Grand Master, Magnan was not a Freemason!

(Napoleon's motive in having Magnan installed as Grand Master was to have him monitor the GODF for any signs of subversion against the Emperor's regime. No definitive records indicate Magnan ever officially became a Mason; however he did claim having higher degrees and also became involved with the suspect Ancient and

Primitive Rite of Masonry — "Memphis-Mizraim," helping to establish the "Sovereign Sanctuary of America, 33-95°.")

Brother Wilson's Sewing Machine

Allen B. Wilson, Harmony Lodge 42, Waterbury, Connecticut, was a cabinet maker by trade, who, in 1850, submitted a patent to improve the primitive sewing machine Elias Howe had invented four years earlier. Considered the first practical sewing machine, Wilson's adaptation enabled him to establish Wheeler & Wilson Manufacturing, which produced its award winning and enormously popular machines. Unbelievably, Brother Wilson designed this amazing product without ever having seen a sewing machine.

Never on Sunday

In 1920, Gate City Lodge 522, Kansas City, met every single day except Sundays, conferring an average of over 21 degrees a week, for a record 1,107 degrees.

The Forgotten Candidate

John W. Davis, Herman Lodge 6 of Clarksburg, West Virginia, is the nearly-forgotten 1924 candidate for President, losing to Calvin Coolidge. His Democratic party was so fractured it took 11 days and 103 ballots to nominate him. The train wreck that was his convention carried forward to his candidacy. Brother Davis was the last of the Jeffersonian conservatives in the Democratic party. His nomination split the Democrats and Coolidge clobbered him by a margin of over 25%, one of the largest ever. Prior to his candidacy, Brother Davis became the only non-British Freemason to serve as the Senior Grand Warden of the Grand Lodge of England.

The Star And Garter

In the Entered Apprentice degree we instruct the candidate that his apron is "more honorable than the Star and Garter." That award or, "The Most Noble Order of the Garter" is a British order of knighthood generally reserved for the gentry. Its membership is limited to the monarch, the Prince of Wales and no more than 24 others. Its badge is an eight-pointed silver star surrounding the cross of St. George, the order's patron saint. Below the knee, the recipient wears a garter bearing the order's French motto "Honi Soit Qui Mal Y Pense," or "Shame on he who thinks evil of this." Only the reigning monarch of England can bestow the order. Although reserved for a select few members of the upper class, it is considered the pinnacle of the honors system in the United Kingdom.

Missouri State Flag

Allen L. Oliver, a member of St. Marks Lodge 93, Cape Girardeau, served as Master of the Missouri Lodge of Research in 1955. He was also President General of the Sons of American Revolution 1946-47 and received the Boy Scouts' prestigious Silver Beaver in 1935. His mother, Marie, designed the Missouri State flag.

A Grave Violation

Hungarian Countess Helene Hadik Barkoczy, sole heir of Count Johann Barkoczy, succeeded him upon his death. She inherited his extensive Masonic library and through it developed an intense interest in the fraternity. The countess sought admittance and using a bit of political influence, was initiated in 1875 in the Lodge Egyenloseg at Unghvar. Upon hearing of this, the Grand Orient of Hungary declared her membership a grave violation of its laws and on January 5, 1876 expelled the Deputy Master of the Lodge and had the names of the officers involved stricken from its roles. Other Lodge members were expelled for up to six months. The Grand Orient proclaimed any Lodge admitting the Countess would be shut down, declared her initiation null and void and demanded the return of her certificate.

Brother James Madison?

James Madison (1751-1836) is usually not considered to be one of the US Presidents who was a Freemason, but strong evidence exists that he was a member. On February 11, 1795, Brother John Francis Mercer, Governor of Maryland, wrote the following to Madison in a letter which still exists in the Library of Congress: "I have had no opportunity of congratulating you before on your becoming a Free Mason — a very ancient and honorable fraternity." John Dove, an early Grand Secretary of the Grand Lodge of Virginia said Madison was one of the original founders of Hiram Lodge 59 in 1800, and became a charter member. On Sept 20, 1817, Madison marched in procession with Charlottesville Lodge 90 and Widow's Son Lodge 60 to lay the cornerstone of Central College at Charlottesville (later the University of Virginia). Perhaps most telling, however, were the attacks made on Madison during the anti-Masonic period. It is safe to conclude just about the only thing not known about the Masonic status of James

Madison — most likely Brother James Madison — is the name of his original Lodge.

The Soldier Without A Smile

Brother Omar Bradley led the D-Day invasion in Normandy June 6, 1944. The soft-spoken general had an accident as a youth, which may have added to the perception he was somewhat shy. While skating at dusk on the lake at Forest Park in Moberly, Missouri, limited visibility caused him to collide with another skater. He described the event as "bone smashing" and said it knocked almost all of his teeth loose, leaving them a jumbled mess. His family had no money for a dentist and he had to live with the resulting bad teeth for the rest of his life. Bradley himself explained that is the reason he is rarely seen smiling in photographs.

Honduras

At least ten Presidents of the Central American republic of Honduras were Freemasons, including: Dionisio Herrera, 1824-1827; Francisco Bertrand, 1913-1915 and 1916-1923; Vincente Tosta, 1924-1925; Miguel Paz Baraona, 1925-1929; Vincente Mejia Colindres, 1929-1933; Juan Manuel Galvez, 1949-1955.

Bad Timing

Thomas A. Smyth, Washington Lodge 1, Wilmington, Delaware, was a Union Brigadier General in the Civil War. Raised March 6, 1865, Brother Smyth was struck by a sniper's bullet on April 7. He died two days later, a short 34 days after becoming a Freemason. He was the last General to die in the conflict, and as he lay dying on April 9, 1865, Ulysses S. Grant sat in a farmhouse 20 miles away, accepting Lee's surrender.

Catch A Man Before You Hang Him

It's common knowledge the "shot heard 'round the world" started the American Revolution. Lesser known is the fact that Commodore Abraham Whipple fired the first shot of the revolution on the water when he captured the British sloop *Rose*. Earlier, in 1772, Whipple also led the first uprising against a British ship when he captured and burned the British schooner *Gaspee*. Whipple and most of his raiding party that overtook the Gaspee were members of St. John's Lodge 1 in Providence, Rhode Island. After the *Rose* incident, the sloop's captain, Sir James Wallace, sent Whipple an angry message: "You, Abraham Whipple, on the 10th of June, 1772, burned His Majesty's vessel, the *Gaspee*, and I will hang you at the yard-arm. ~James Wallace." To this, Brother Whipple replied, "To Sir James Wallace, Sir: Always catch a man before you hang him. ~Abraham Whipple"

Cannons

The firing glasses familiar to Table Lodges have thick bases to protect them from breaking when rapped against the table in unison at the completion of a toast. They are so called because the sound of the glasses hitting the table causes a sound similar to a cannon firing. For this reason many Lodges refer to them as "cannons."

Pesky Punctuation

Harry S. Truman had no middle name. He explained the "S" stood for a combination of both his grandfathers' names (Shippe/Solomon) and he once joked that "S" was his middle name. Unfortunately, when you're the President of the US, people take you seriously. From that offhand remark a controversy developed that continues today, with many contending there should be no period after Brother Truman's middle initial. Truman, no doubt amused by the ruckus, said he had no preference about this, but actions speak louder than words. Virtually every time Brother Harry signed his name or initialed something, he used a period after the letter "S" in the middle. He also used the period in all typewritten documents and even had a signature stamp made which included the period. Although the controversy continues, it seems Brother Truman himself has settled the issue.

The Lowly Paper Cup Saved His Life

Elmer Zebley Taylor (1864-1949), Lodge unknown, invented the paper cup. He marketed his invention under the brand name Kleen Kup through his company, Mono Containers, Ltd., making a fortune. Mono Containers had plants in ten countries so Brother Taylor resided in Europe, but spent summers in New Jersey. Making that trip for the summer of 1912, Brother Taylor booked a cabin on the *Titanic*. His substantial wealth enabled him to travel in a prime first-class cabin, located close to the main deck area. When the ship struck an iceberg, Brother Taylor reacted immediately. He and his wife Juliet reached the lifeboats before the crew began prohibiting men to board them. As a result, he boarded and became one of the very few adult males to survive the tragedy. In a way the lowly paper cup, which had enabled him to amass the wealth to afford that prime cabin close to the main deck and lifeboats, saved his life.

Guthrie

The iconic Guthrie Scottish Rite Building sits on grounds once designated for the Oklahoma State Capitol building.

The Elevators That Run Sideways

In order to have unbroken floor space, the elevators in Alexandria's George Washington Memorial run sideways 35 feet as they rise 244 feet in 2 slanting shafts from the main floor to the observation deck. At the time the memorial was built, this was considered an engineering marvel, and even today remains somewhat unique in the field of architecture.

The Anti-Mason Who Was A Freemason

William Wirt, first presidential candidate of the Anti-Masonic party was, in fact, a Freemason. He even defended the order in his acceptance speech at the convention.

Charmed

In 1877, a miner prospecting near Mt. Rushmore established a gold mine. At a loss to name the mine, he noticed the York Rite Chapter charm on his watch chain and called it the Keystone mine. The town of Keystone, SD ("The home of Mt. Rushmore") was named after the mine, its name therefore originating from a Masonic watch charm.

Washington's Masonic Courtesy

When the British retreated after a skirmish in the revolutionary war, American troops found Masonic regalia and a book of constitutions left in the encampment the British had abandoned. General Washington himself returned the Masonic artifacts to the British troops, under a flag of truce, accompanied by an escort and a guard of honor.

Named In Honor Of A Saint

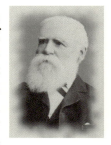

John Ellis (1835-1913), was a Canadian Statesman and journalist and a member of Lodge of Social & Military Virtues, Montreal. He served as Grand Master of New Brunswick, Grand High Priest of the Grand Chapter of New Brunswick, Grand Master of the Grand Council of Maritime Provinces, Supreme Grand Master of the Sovereign Great Priory of Canada and Sovereign Grand Commander of the Scottish Rite in Canada. He was named in honor of the saint celebrated on his birthday, February 14. His full name is John Valentine Ellis.

Alfred P. Murrah

The Alfred P. Murrah Federal Building, destroyed April 19, 1995, in the Oklahoma City bombing, was named in honor of a Freemason. Brother Murrah, of Capital City Lodge 518 in Oklahoma City, was a judge who pioneered the practices of pretrial conferences and litigation panels. Brother Earl Warren described him as "one of the foremost figures in the American judiciary."

Hands Clasped Forever

Francis, 2nd Earl of Moira (1754-1826) was a British soldier and colonial administrator, born Francis Rawdon Hastings. From 1790 until 1813, he was Acting Grand Master to H.R.H. George, Prince of Wales, later George IV and, in 1806-1807, he served as Grand Master of Scotland. He is credited with saving Freemasonry in England when he worked to defeat the Unlawful Societies Act of 1799, which would have required the dissolution of the order. Upon his death, he was buried in Malta, but left an unusual request. His wish was that, prior to his burial, his "right hand might be cut off" and buried with his wife at her death. His wish was granted and his hand now rests clasped in hers, buried in the family vault in the Old Kirk of Loudoun.

Lifesaver

Legend has it that Brother John Hobert owed his life to this Masonic ring. Brother Hobert, a Union soldier, was captured during the Civil War and imprisoned at the notorious Confederate prison at Andersonville. A Brother Mason noticed his ring. As a result, Brother Hobert was released and sent back home to Iowa. Brother Hobert gave the ring to a Lodge Brother who, in turn, left it to Oney Kirby, his son and Brother Mason. The ring is on display at the Masonic Museum in Columbia, Missouri.

Robert & Josephine Perry

In order to prepare for exploring the north pole, Brother Robert Peary first made an expedition to Greenland. During this training expedition Peary, a member of Kane Lodge 454 in New York, experienced the same grueling conditions he knew he would face in his Arctic adventure. In the process he discovered Independence Bay, explored the entire frigid northern coast and reached Greenland's northernmost point, Cape Morris Jessup. Amazingly, Peary's pregnant wife Josephine accompanied him on the trip.

First Stone

July 4, 1828, the Grand Lodge of Maryland laid the "first stone" for the Baltimore & Ohio Railroad. Charles Carroll, last surviving signatory of the Declaration of Independence, presided. The stone is now located in the B&O Railroad Museum, Baltimore.

Tipperary

The inspirational World War I battle song *It's A Long Way To Tipperary* was first sung in public at a Ladies Night in York Lodge, Toronto, Ontario on March 27, 1912.

First Photograph of a President in Office

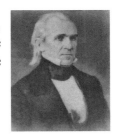

On February 14, 1849, Brother James K. Polk, Columbia Lodge 31, Columbia, Tennessee, became the first President of the United States to be photographed while in office.

The Family Secret

Major General Wayne C. Smith was raised in Schofield Lodge 443, Schofield Barracks, Hawaii and later became charter Master of Fort Campbell Lodge 946 of Fort Campbell, Kentucky. He is the only military general other than George Washington known to be a charter Master of a Lodge. He had an impressive list of Masonic accomplishments including a term as National President of Sojourners, 1956-57. His father was not a Mason and he did not learn of his grandfather's membership until his mother was on her deathbed. Amazingly the reason for both was the same: family fears of repercussions from his great-great-grandfather's involvement in the Morgan affair more than a century earlier.

Posthumous Fame

Peter Marshall (1902-1949), Old Monkland St. James Lodge 177, Coatbridge, Scotland was a Presbyterian minister who served twice as Chaplain of the US Senate. Although a man of accomplishment, he was never widely known until after his untimely death, when his wife Catherine wrote his biography, *A Man Called Peter*, a best-seller which made him world famous.

The Father Of Yellowstone

Cornelius Hedges (1831-1907) had an outstanding Masonic career. Master of Helena Lodge 3, he was active in the York Rite and served as Grand Secretary of Montana. Brother Hedges was an attorney who became a state senator, was an editorial writer for the Helena Herald and founded the Helena public library system. He is best remembered, however, for being a part of the first expedition to Yellowstone and for suggesting the US make Yellowstone a national park. Today, he continues to be known as "The Father of Yellowstone."

Historic Gavel

After his historic flight across the Atlantic Ocean, Charles Lindbergh gave this gavel to his Masonic Lodge, Keystone Lodge 243, St. Louis. The gavel is made from the wood propeller of Lindbergh's famous plane, "The Spirit of St. Louis," and is now on display in the Masonic Museum in Columbia, Missouri.

Washington's Constitution

On June 22, 2012, Brother George Washington's personal copy of the US Constitution sold at auction for $9.8 million, a record for any American book or historic document. The document contains Washington's personal annotations regarding his thoughts on the Constitution and Bill of Rights. The non-profit Mount Vernon Ladies Association of the Union purchased the document, which is in book form and in near-pristine condition. The new owners plan to keep it in Washington's library at Mt. Vernon.

Three-Finger Brown

Mordecai Brown (1876-1949), a member of Edward Dobbins Lodge 164, Lawrenceville, Illinois, was Elected to Baseball's Hall of Fame in 1949. He was a standout Chicago Cubs pitcher who won 20 or more games for six straight seasons. In 1908 as a fielding pitcher he did not commit a single error and pitched a record four shutout games in a row. Prior to becoming a major-leaguer, he was injured in a coal mining accident which severed the index finger and severely deformed the middle finger on his pitching hand. Amazingly, he amassed his spectacular pitching record with the missing finger and deformed hand, earning him his nickname, "Three Finger" Brown.

Interestingly, in a time when physical deformities might block someone from Masonic membership, Brother Brown's petition required review by a District Deputy Grand Master, who had to approve his admission to the fraternity.

Mauritius Cathedral

Francis Edward Rawdon-Hastings, Second Earl of Moira became British Governor General of India in 1813. He served as 46th Grand Master of Masons of Scotland in 1806-07 and Acting Grand Master to H.R.H. George, Prince of Wales 1790-1813. Upon leaving to become Governor General, the Grand Lodge also appointed him Acting Grand Master of India. He set sail for his new post and along the way made port on the small island of Mauritius, east of Madagascar. There, at the request of the citizens of

Port Louis, who had learned of his credentials, he laid the cornerstone of the town's new Catholic Cathedral, which is still in use.

Variety Is The Spice Of Life (And Dating)

Brother Will Rogers dated all seven of the Blake sisters before asking the youngest, Betty, to marry him in 1906. Betty, apprehensive about a life in show business, turned him down. A year and a half later the persistent Rogers changed her mind and they married. Betty met Will when he was, what else, on a date with one of her older sisters.

Charles Dickens Lodge

Author Charles Dickens was a resolute anti-Mason, yet there once was a Charles Dickens Lodge in Chigwell, Essex, England.

Master

Most Worshipful Brother Harry S. Truman served as Master of the Missouri Lodge of Research while he was also President of the United States, in 1950.

The First Environmental Protest Song

A Freemason wrote what some claim is the first environmental protest song. George P. Morris, St. John's 1, NY, wrote *Woodman Spare That Tree* as a poem in 1837 and later that year it became a popular song. While some claim its status as the first environmental protest song, others point out the theme of the work is merely that of someone sentimentally trying to save a single tree remembered from his youth.

Return Jonathan Meigs

Return Jonathan Meigs, Sr. (1740-1823), American Revolution Colonel, was a founding settler of Ohio and an Indian Agent in Tennessee. His son, Return Jonathan Meigs, Jr. (1764-1824) served as Governor of Ohio and US Postmaster General. Both were members of American Union Lodge 1 in Ohio. The elder served as Master in 1801. He was the son of Return Meigs and grandson of Jana Meigs, both with an unknown Masonic status. Their unusual names came from Grandpa Jana's frustrations in pursuing the woman who ultimately became his wife, Hannah Willard. Hanna was a Puritan who refused to marry Jana on many occasions. Jana gave it one final try and upon being refused again, gave up and mounted his horse to ride off. At that, Hannah, realizing she was losing him forever, called out, "Return, Jana, return!" Jana did return and the couple was married May 16, 1698. Jana said when she cried out to him, "Return" was the sweetest word he had ever heard, and named his son Return in honor of it, the name being passed down afterward.

A Cup Formed From A Skull

English romantic poet George Gordon Byron, 6th Baron Byron, is known today simply as "Lord Byron." Historians suspect he may have become a Freemason during the time he stayed in Italy; however, his Masonic status remains unconfirmed. What is known of him, among other things, is the personal cup from which he drank was made from a human skull. Lord  Byron wrote of the cup in his poem *Lines Inscribed Upon a Cup Formed From a Skull* and elsewhere had this to say about it, "The gardener in digging discovered a skull... Observing it to be of giant size and in a perfect state of preservation, a strange fancy seized me of having it set and mounted as a drinking cup."

War And Peace

It is said more people have falsely claimed to have read the book *War and Peace* than any other. In that book, Count Leo Tolstoy (1828-1910) mentions Freemasonry no less than 89 times, includes several characters who are Freemasons. and describes a Masonic initiation  in such detail that many assume he was a Freemason. In fact, no record of his membership exists and it is unlikely he ever became a member. For most of his life Freemasonry was forbidden in Russia and by the time it returned, he was old and in poor health.

Prince Hall

 On March 6, 1775, Prince Hall and 14 other African American men were made Master Masons in a British Army Lodge of Irish register. The Lodge gave them the privilege of meeting, marching in procession,

and burying their dead, but not conferring degrees. In March, 1784, Hall petitioned the Grand Lodge of England for a charter which was issued September 29, 1784, but was not delivered until April 29, 1787, establishing African Lodge 459 on May 6, 1787. Four years later, on June 24, 1791, the African Grand Lodge was formed with Prince Hall as Grand Master. MWB Hall died December 7, 1807. Subsequently, in his honor, the Lodge became M.W. Prince Hall Grand Lodge, F&AM, of Massachusetts. Today, the great majority of US state Grand Lodges as well as the Grand Lodge of England and many international Grand Lodges recognize Prince Hall Lodges.

Brother Who Banned Freemasonry — Twice

Alexander I (1777-1825) Czar of Russia was a member of Canongate Kilwinning Lodge of Edinburgh, Scotland and a member of the Polish Grand Orient. Polish Masons gave a banquet in his honor in 1815, and Alexander was a generous donor to the group. Previously, upon becoming Czar in 1801, he almost immediately banned Freemasonry. However, Johann Boeber, who later was Grand Master of Russia, convinced him of the good works of Freemasonry. Alexander not only rescinded his ban, but also became a member. Then, over 20 years later, he again became suspicious of Freemasonry and banned it for a second time August 1, 1822.

Strange Bedfellows

Brother Roscoe Turner, 32° (1895–1970), Corinth Lodge 116, Corinth, Mississippi, was a pioneer American flier. Congress awarded him the Distinguished Flying Cross in 1952 but, unbelievably, the military turned down his application to become a pilot in World War I. After serving as a driver in the war, Turner went on to become the country's top barnstorming ace, operated the world's first high speed airline and held almost every air speed record of his day. The public, however, probably best knew him as the barnstorming pilot who traveled the country with his pet lion. The lion, Gilmore, was a promotion for the Gilmore Oil Company, which used a lion as its symbol. Turner was said even to sleep in the same room with Gilmore and pictures, perhaps staged, may support the claim.

A 30 - 1 Longshot

George McManus (1884-1954), was the creator of the comic strip "Bringing Up Father," as well as other world famous comic series. A member of Dirigo Lodge 30, New York City, Brother McManus funded the start to his astonishing career by wagering $100 on a 30-1 longshot horse and winning.

The Christmas Flower

Brother Joel R. Poinsett (1779-1851) had a successful diplomatic career as US Secretary of War, US Congressman and Minister to Mexico. Additionally, he was instrumental in the formation of the Grand Lodge of Mexico, served as Deputy General Grand High Priest of the General Grand Chapter of Royal Arch Masons, Master of two of his Lodges, Deputy Grand Master of the Grand Lodge of South Carolina and Grand High Priest of the Grand Chapter of South Carolina. Even with impressive credentials like that, however, he is best remembered for a plant he brought back from Mexico, the Mexican Fire Plant. After cultivating it and introducing it in the US, the plant was named in his honor. Today, the Poinsettia is the traditional Christmas flower.

Try, Try Again

Sir Thomas J. Lipton, a member of Lodge Scotia 178 in Glasgow Scotland, was known worldwide as the founder of Lipton Tea. The company bearing his name even today remains a global business titan. Lesser known is the fact that Brother Lipton was also the most persistent participant in the America's Cup yachting series history. He invested millions of dollars building five yachts, all named *Shamrock*. In spite of his sizable investment and perseverance, he lost every race.

The Washington Medallion

Struck in 1797, the Washington Medallion commemorated the just-completed presidency of Brother George Washington. It bore his likeness on the obverse with the simple text, "Washington President." The real purpose of the medallion, however, became apparent upon viewing the reverse side, which showed the working tools and symbols of a Masonic Lodge. The initials at the bottom, "GWGGM" stood for "George Washington General Grand Master." The coin actually was a promotional piece advocating the election of Brother Washington as General Grand Master of Masons in America, representing one of the several campaigns to organize a general Grand Lodge, all of which failed

Standout Soldier, Simple Grave

Audie Murphy, North Hollywood Lodge 542, California, was World War II's most decorated soldier. As a Medal of Honor recipient, he could have had his Arlington Cemetery gravestone gilded, but instead chose to have a plain stone, no different from those of his fellow soldiers.  Still, aside from John Kennedy, Brother Murphy's grave is the most visited site at Arlington. So many people come to see his grave the cemetery had to build a special walkway leading to it.

Giving Thanks For The Constitution

The first official national "Thanksgiving Day," established on November 26, 1789, was originally created by George Washington for "giving thanks for the Constitution."

Initiated Passed And Raised On His Deathbed

Presbyterian clergyman Moses D. Hoge was said to have been the most eloquent speaker in the southern Presbyterian church. Lodge 51, Richmond, Virginia, initiated him into all three degrees November 22, 1898 and appointed him Lodge Chaplain. The entire ceremony took place in his bedroom with Brother Hoge on his deathbed. Lodge minutes reported the Grand Master of Virginia, R.T.W. Duke, Jr. conferred the degrees, "dispensing with such portions of the ceremony as in his opinion the physical condition of the candidate required." Brother Hoge passed away 45 days later, January 6, 1899.

The Brother Who Invaded Canada

Lucius V. Bierce was a member of Akron Lodge 83 and served as Grand Master of Ohio in 1854. Sensing discord among Canadians manifested by scattered rebellions, and holding a strong belief in the interest of liberty he determined to help his neighbors to the north. In 1838 he led a band of followers from Detroit into Windsor, Ontario, and attacked Canada! His battle cry was, "Save Canadians from the Crown!" Unfortunately for MWB Bierce, the vast majority of Canadians did not want to be saved, and they quickly defeated his well-intentioned militia.

Bambi

The Book *Bambi — A Life In The Woods*, by Brother Felix Salten (Salzmann), a member of Lodge Zur Wahrheit in Vienna, received almost universal acclaim not only as a children's novel, but also as a symbolic statement on certain aspects of the human condition. More commonly known simply as *Bambi*, the book today is considered a literary classic as is its animated adaptation by Walt Disney. Nazi Germany, however, banned the book as "political allegory on the treatment of Jews in Europe." So many copies of the book were burned there that today, first edition copies are extremely rare.

Ringling Brothers

The minutes of Baraboo Lodge 34, Baraboo Wisconsin, from April 8, 1891 read as follows: "A special meeting was called to hear a report of a committee relative to the purchase of a lot where the temple now stands. The meeting was opened by the regular officers, after which the following assumed the chairs: WM, Alf T. Ringling; SW, August Ringling; JW, Al Ringling; SD, Charles Ringling; JD, Otto Ringling; and SS, Henry Ringling." The Ringlings, along with their other brothers and father were ardent Masons. Together, the brothers owned a business you may be familiar with — The Ringling Brother's Circus.

The Great Moon Hoax Of 1835

Long before Percival Lowell claimed to have discovered evidence of civilization on Mars, or before Orson Wells frightened the country with a mock Martian invasion, legitimate scientists in the 1830s were concocting extravagant claims of the possibility of a civilization on the moon. In response to what he felt were the ridiculous claims, Brother Richard A. Locke (Benevolent Lodge 28, New York) fabricated a story about the discovery of lunar inhabitants so plausible many scientists of the day endorsed it. Using the name "Sir John Herschel," Locke published the "discovery" in a series of articles in the *New York Sun* (where he was a reporter) in 1835, causing a national sensation. He let the story linger for six weeks before revealing it was a satiric way of ridiculing the outlandish "scientific" claims of his day, amidst charges he had only written the series of articles to increase circulation.

The Gun Invented To Save Lives

A member of Center Lodge 23 in Indianapolis, he invented a screw propeller for steamboats, a rice sewing machine, a wheat drill and various items which improved the operation of toilets, bicycles, steam cleaning machines and pneumatic devices. But Dr. Richard Gatling (1818 – 1903) is remembered almost exclusively for a single invention. It was a rotating barrel, rapid fire gun which bears his name: the Gatling gun. Dr. Gatling was a physician who never practiced medicine, but invented the deadly weapon for the sole purpose of SAVING lives. He felt the existence of such a destructive gun would reduce the need for large armies and save lives caused by the destruction of war and its accompanying diseases.

To Confuse Future Archaeologists

A massive 67-foot statue of Brother Sam Houston stands north of Houston in Huntsville, Texas. At its completion, the concrete mixer used for assembly was placed inside the statue at the position of Brother Houston's heart. According to the museum curator at the site, "They did that just to confuse future archaeologists."

Famous Last Words

Georges Jacques Danton (1759-1794), a member of the Lodge of the Nine Sisters at Paris, was a French revolutionary leader who advocated a unified France and stable republican government. Caught up in the "Reign of Terror," Danton went to prison and the guillotine at the order of the dictator Robespierre. As Brother Danton's tumbrel carried him to his execution, it rolled past Robespierre's house with Danton shouting insults at the tyrant and predicting he would also be executed... which he was. When the executioner took him up to the guillotine, Brother Danton turned to him and uttered some of history's most famous last words, "You will show my head to the crowd: It is worth seeing."

Strongman Lodge

Thomas Topham was an 18th century Englishman famous for feats of incredible strength. Brother Topham was a pub owner who was so strong he could roll up a pewter dish in the same manner a normal person could roll up a piece of paper. Known for being able to brace himself against a stone fence and out-pull two horses straining against him on the other side, his Lodge was named Strongman Lodge in his honor. The sign above the Lodge door showed him pulling against the horses.

Child Prodigy

Austrian composer Wolfgang Amadeus Mozart (1756-1791) was a member of Lodge Zur neugekroentin, Hoffnung (new crowned hope). Renowned as a musical genius and composer of pieces with Masonic themes, Mozart was a child prodigy who composed his first published works at the age of seven. In 1770, at the age of 14, he heard Gregorio Allegri's *Miserere* a single time, went home and wrote the entire piece down from memory.

The Texas State Flag

Brothers Lorenzo DeZavala (Independence Lodge 3) and David G. Burnet (Holland Lodge 1) designed early versions of what is now the Texas state flag. In 1839, Texas Republic President Mirabeau B. Lamar (Harmony Lodge 6 of Galveston) commissioned Brother Charles B. Stewart (Montgomery Lodge 25) to design the state flag that flies over Texas today.

Brother Saves Albert Pike's Home

During a Union attack on Little Rock, Arkansas, Union General Thomas Hart Benton ordered his troops to guard the home of Albert Pike to protect the Masonic Library there. Benton at the time was Grand Master of Iowa, serving in that office from 1861-63.

Benton was also the nephew of Missouri's first senator and Masonic Brother Thomas Hart Benton.

The World's Only Anti-Masonic Monument

The world's only anti-Masonic monument is located in Batavia Cemetery in New York. Batavia was the home of the infamous William Morgan. Morgan's full Masonic status is in doubt but it is certain he was initiated into Royal Arch Masonry. In 1826, he announced he would publish the secrets of the fraternity. A zealous group of Freemasons, in an attempt to prevent that, kidnapped Morgan and purportedly killed him. Morgan's fate remains a mystery. Some believe he is buried at the location of this monument, but the fact is he disappeared after the kidnapping and, despite rumors, was never seen again. The 20-foot marker in Batavia is only a memorial, not a gravestone.

The Bloody Massacre

Paul Revere, Grand Master of Massachusetts from 1794-97, is one of the most famous of the American Revolution patriots. Immortalized in the Henry Wadsworth poem, *The Midnight Ride of Paul Revere*, Brother Revere was also a participant in the Boston Tea Party, a soldier, arms manufacturer and renowned silversmith. Lesser known is the fact that his artwork extended beyond his silver pieces. He is also the creator of the famous engraving *The Bloody Massacre* depicting the Boston Massacre of March 5, 1770, where British Troops killed five civilian men, including Crispus Attucks, a former slave, generally regarded as the first person killed in the Revolution. The engraving also includes a poem written by Brother Revere, *Unhappy Boston*.

Sharpshooters

Christian Sharps, a member of Meridian Sun Lodge 58 in Philadelphia, was a machinist who invented the famous Sharps breech-loading rifle in 1848. An important part of the Civil War, the iconic rifle was used by Colonel Hiram Berdan's elite regiment. Owing to the weapons they used, these expert riflemen earned the name "Berdan's Sharpshooters," originating the term still in common use to designate a highly skilled marksman: sharpshooter.

Tower Of London

Originally built as a royal residence, the infamous Tower of London is better known as a gruesome prison. At various times the Tower imprisoned Freemasons (e.g., American Revolutionary statesman Henry Laurens) and at other times was managed by our Brothers (e.g., Paul Sanford, 3rd Baron Methuen and Frederic Augustus Thesiger). In a unique event on June 3, 1938, while its members were guarding the Tower, Lodge Glittering Star 322, an Irish military Lodge, conferred a first degree.

Arnold Palmer — Tennis Star?

In 1974, Arnold Palmer, professional golfer, Loyalhanna Lodge 275 of Labrobe, Pennsylvania, made a Cadillac commercial featuring his skills as, what else — a tennis player. Brother Palmer's tennis game, the commercial and 1974 Cadillac sales all proved to be lackluster. In subsequent endorsements when it has come to sports, Brother Palmer has limited his activities to something he's pretty good at... golf.

Ronald Reagan

Ronald Reagan (1911 - 2004) was not a Freemason. However, in February, 1988, a group of Masonic leaders, including the Grand Master of DC, met with him and made him an honorary member of the Shrine and Scottish Rite.

Grand Master In Two Hemispheres

Dr. Carlos Rodriguez Jimenez served as the Grand Master of two countries. He was Grand Master of the Grand Lodge of Venezuela in 1947, and then served as Japan's first Grand Master beginning in 1957.

A Nice Sentiment

George Washington, Alexandria Lodge 22, and James Monroe, Williamsburgh Lodge 6, both in Virginia, were the only two United States Presidents elected essentially without opposition. In 1820, all members of the Electoral College were obligated to cast a vote for Monroe but New Hampshire representative William Plumer instead voted for John Quincy Adams. A popular story is that Plumer cast the renegade vote against Monroe because he felt no president except Washington should garner a unanimous vote in the Electoral College. While this is a nice sentiment, it's probably not true. Plumer was not a supporter of Monroe. More than that, however, Plumer was also charged to vote for Brother Monroe's Vice Presidential candidate. Monroe's pick for Vice President was Daniel Tompkins, a member of Hiram Lodge 72, Mt. Pleasant, NY who later served as that state's Grand Master. Plumer detested Tompkins, describing him as as "grossly intemperate" and having "not that weight of character which his office requires." It is more likely it was Monroe's association with Brother Tompkins, rather than Plumer's admiration of Washington, that cost Monroe a unanimous election.

Mickey Mouse, DeMolay

Walt Disney (1901-1966) was not a Freemason, but he was always supportive of the fraternity sponsoring, among other things a Magic Kingdom Mason's club for the employees in his parks. Disney was, however, an enthusiastic DeMolay. He was the 107th young boy initiated  into the order, was a member of the Mother Chapter, had a lifelong relationship with Frank Land and was ultimately inducted into DeMolay's Legion of Honor as well as its Hall of Fame. Walt endorsed making the iconic Mickey Mouse an honorary member of DeMolay — the only such use of Mickey he ever allowed — and then, in the 1930s a mysterious set of comic strips appeared depicting Mickey organizing a Barnyard DeMolay Chapter for publication in the DeMolay magazine. No one ever determined who created the comics, but speculation includes the fact it may have been Walt himself, who personally signed them.

The Versatile Patriot

Brother Thomas McKean was the only member of the Continental congress who served from the time it opened until the end of the American Revolution (1774-89). He was the second president of that body in 1781, earning him the designation by some standards as the "second President of the  United States." In 1777, he added to those responsibilities by serving as both President of Delaware and Chief Justice of the Pennsylvania supreme court. He signed the Declaration of Independence but... oops... a printer's error left his name off the document distributed to the public. Amazingly, in 1776, this versatile patriot wrote the constitution of the state of Delaware in a single night.

The Rifle That Served For 70 Years

Odus Creamer Horney (1866-1957), Alamo Lodge 44, San Antonio, was an armed forces officer who eventually attained the rank of Brigadier General. A tinkerer by nature, he developed a new, more comfortable and durable riding saddle for the military. Then, not satisfied with the standard issue rifle, he designed and built a new model which became the US military's most famous standard issue weapon. His invention, the Springfield Rifle M1903 was so good it was the standard issue from 1905 through World War II and, although finally replaced by the M1, remained the army's sniper rifle through that conflict, Korea and even Viet Nam, in an astonishing run of nearly 70 years.

The Sad And Curious Case Of Brother Gloyd

Brother Charles Gloyd was a successful western Missouri physician who, among other things, organized and became first Master of Holden Lodge 262 in Johnson County, Missouri, in 1867. That same year, Brother Gloyd's mother began caring for an infant living with a young girl in town, Carrie Moore. Charles and Carrie met through that relationship, fell in love and married. Unfortunately, Brother Gloyd had been hiding his dependence on alcohol. The marriage soon fell apart and Dr. Gloyd died less than a year later. The tragedy devastated young Carrie, who was certain her husband's alcoholism was at the root of the problem. She remarried, took her second husband's surname and changed the spelling of her first name to "Carry." With an ax in one hand and a Bible in the other, she dedicated her life to eliminating the scourge of alcoholism and showing demon rum it had better not mess with the likes of Carry A. Nation.

There is some controversy over the spelling of Ms. Nation's first name. Her father recorded it as "Carry" in the family Bible, but official records show it as "Carrie." Nation used "Carrie" most of her life but once her anti-alcohol movement was in full swing she saw the value of the slogan-like name "Carry A. Nation." She adopted that as her official name and even had it trademarked. That is also how it appears on her tombstone in Belton, Missouri.

Liberty Bell

The Liberty Bell cracked while tolling the death of Brother John Marshall, 4th Chief Justice of the US Supreme Court and Grand Master of Virginia from 1793-95.

Henry Knox Lodge

After the *USS Constitution* ("Old Ironsides") was restored and moored in Charlestown Naval Shipyard (Boston), a Masonic Lodge, Henry Knox Lodge of Massachusetts, was constituted on the ship on March 17, 1926.

Oldest US Masonic Building

Mason's Hall on Franklin Street in Richmond Virginia is the oldest Masonic building in the US built specifically as a Masonic meeting place. It has been used continuously and is the home of Richmond Lodge 10. Due to the destruction of the Civil War, it remains one of the few buildings surviving from 18th century

Richmond. It would not be there today except for a Union General, a Freemason, who ordered it to be protected from fire.

Persistent Stories

Stories persist that Charles Lindbergh, a member of Keystone Lodge 243 in St. Louis, wore a square and compasses sewn on his jacket, and also had a square and compasses attached to his plane's dashboard on his famous flight across the Atlantic. Most likely, neither is true. Photographs taken of Lindbergh on the day of his flight show nothing sewn on his jacket. Also, the few existing pictures of his plane's cockpit from that era show no square and compasses.

David's Temple?

King David wanted to build the original temple, but the Lord refused because David was a man of war: "But the word of the LORD came to me, saying, Thou hast shed blood abundantly, and hast made great wars: thou  shalt not build an house unto my name, because thou hast shed much blood upon the earth in my sight" (1 Chronicles 22:8 KJV). David did, however provide the design for the temple (1 Chronicles 29:2-6) and also some of the funding. The cost of the temple in today's dollars is estimated to be $3 to $6 billion.

Hemiciclio a Juarez

Masonic Brothers, Benito Juarez (1806-1872) and Porfino Diaz (1830-1915) were comrades in arms who had fought together during the French intervention in Mexico. Afterward, however, when Juarez became President of Mexico, they became bitter political enemies and Diaz unsuccessfully attempted to unseat Juarez in what some historians term a revolt. The relationship between the Brothers eased gradually and eventually Diaz became President. When Juarez died, Diaz erected an elaborate monument in his honor, despite the strained relationship they had once shared. The monument, Hemiciclio a Juarez, is considered one of the most magnificent in metropolitan Mexico City and serves as a gateway to Alameda Central Park.

The Magic Flute

Wolfgang Amadeus Mozart composed his epic opera, *The Magic Flute* in 1791, while a member of the Viennese Masonic Lodge "Zur Wohltätigkeit" ("Beneficence"). Brother Mozart authored the work with its several Masonic allegories to ensure the enlightenment of the Craft would survive the Austrian emperor's tyrannic reign which, among other things, banned Masonic initiations.

Helicopter Mom

Mary Pinkney Hardy MacArthur may have been the world's first and, in fact, most obsessive "helicopter parent." When her son, Douglas MacArthur, Manila Lodge 1, Philippines, went to West Point, Pinky, as she was called, went with him, rented an apartment with a view of his room and spied on him with a telescope to make sure he was studying!

The Prince Of Wales In Missouri

On September 26, 1860, Albert Edward, Prince of Wales, future Grand Master of the Grand Lodge of England and later King Edward VII (1901-10), visited St. Louis and attended the Missouri agricultural and mechanical fair. There he purchased a trotting horse and dined on buffalo tongue, quail, prairie chicken and Missouri wine.

On The Highest Hills And In The Lowest Vales

Traditionally ancient Masons met "on the highest hills and in the lowest vales" to ensure privacy. In an attempt to continue that tradition, Masonic Lodges have sought out unique places to hold special communications. Two such meetings in particular seem to be the record holders in this regard.

On April 10, 1936, the Brothers of Winnedumah Lodge 287 of Bishop, California, held a meeting near the lowest point in the United

States in Death Valley National Park. Members of 50 Lodges from 10 surrounding states joined the gathering at 270 feet below sea level.

On the other side of the spectrum, in 1910, Cascade Lodge 5 of Banff, Alberta, Canada met west of Calgary near the summit of Mt. Aylmer. Held at an elevation of 3161 meters or 10,371 feet, 18 Lodge members and 13 visitors attended.

The Blue Ribbon

Judges at the Colombian Exposition in 1893 declared Brother Frederick Pabst's brew as the best beer at the event, also known as the Chicago World's Fair. Brother Pabst, Aurora Lodge 30, Milwaukee, won a gold medal for his formula but not, as many think, a blue ribbon. The name of his beer, "Pabst Blue Ribbon," comes from his company's practice of tying (then later sealing) a blue ribbon on the neck of every single bottle of beer he produced from 1882 until 1916.

Critically Acclaimed Artist

Sir Winston Churchill, Rosemary Lodge 2581, London, is well-known as a statesman, author, speaker and historian. As Prime Minister, he led England through its darkest days of World War II and served a second term as the cold war took root in the early to mid 1950s. In 1946, during a landmark speech in Fulton Missouri, he warned about the approaching tensions between western and communist block countries and originated the term "iron curtain." Less known

At the Pyramids
by Winston Churchill

about Brother Churchill is the fact that he was an accomplished artist. Having started painting late in life without formal training, Churchill created oil paintings which have won critical acclaim and commanded handsome prices.

President And Chief Justice

William Howard Taft was a member of Kilwinning Lodge 365, Cincinnati, Ohio. He was the 27th President of the United States (1909-1913) and served as Chief Justice of the US Supreme Court (1921-1930) making him the only person ever to serve in the highest positions of both the executive and judicial branches of our government.

Frenzy Of Persecution

Aaron Burr was disgraced and politically ruined when, as Vice President of the US, he killed Alexander Hamilton in an illegal duel. Subsequently, Burr conspired to seize territory in the Southwest and declare himself Emperor of the country he planned to establish there. Burr's co-conspirator, James Wilkinson, Governor of Northern Louisiana Territory and Commander-in-Chief of the US Army, betrayed him. Authorities then captured Burr and tried him for treason. Acquitted on a technicality, Burr fled to Europe. Burr was never a Freemason; however, in their frenzy of persecution following the Morgan Affair, anti-Masons not only claimed Burr was a member of the fraternity, but also insisted he used the Royal Arch cipher as a coded method of communicating with his co-conspirators.

Dues Paid In Full

Tom Mix, early cowboy movie superstar, was raised a Master Mason at Utopia Lodge 537 of Los Angeles on February 21, 1925. He was so excited about becoming a Freemason that, in a day prior to life endowments, he immediately paid the dues for his first ten years of membership.

Unchristian Conduct

The Presbyterian Church in 1831, sanctioned Nathaniel Beverley Tucker (1784-1851), second Grand Master of the Grand Lodge of Missouri, for "unchristian conduct." Certain parties, it seems, claimed he "partook of the amusement of dancing" on three occasions. There is no record of any action taken against him, but shortly thereafter MWB Tucker became an Episcopalian.

103 Days

Brother James K. Polk, 11th president of the United States, Columbia Lodge 31, Columbia, Tennessee, left office on March 4, 1849 and died June 15, 1849, just 103 days later. He had the shortest retirement of any US President and, at 53, was also the youngest President to die in retirement.

The Good Luck Charm

Brother William McKinley, 25th President of the United States loved carnations and considered them good luck. On September 6, 1901, McKinley gave his good luck charm, a red carnation that he was wearing, to a little girl in the receiving line at the Pan-American Exposition. Seconds later, an assassin struck, shooting him and wounding him fatally.

An Ironic Twist

Freiherr vom Stein Schule in Fulda, Germany is a high school named in honor of Heinrich Friedrich Karl vom Stein (1737-1851), a Prussian statesmen whose progressive reforms resulted in the unification of Germany. The school originally was to have been named in honor of Karl Ferdinand Braun, a pioneer in radio and television technology;  however, some local citizens discovered Braun was a Freemason and demanded a different name for the school. Wanting to avoid a dispute, city fathers obliged and named the school for vom Stein. Later it was discovered that Braun was, indeed, not a Freemason. In an ironic twist, it was also discovered that the school's namesake was in fact Brother vom Stein, a member of the lodge "Joseph of the Three Helmets" at Wetzlar, Germany.

Strange Inheritance

In 1884, Eastland Lodge 467, Texas, inherited an estate from a recently departed Brother. The inheritance included the Brother's farm, belongings and livestock as well as John and Nathan Tracy, both of his sons! The transaction was legal and administered by T.H. Connor, Chief Justice of the Second Court of Appeals. In 1932, Nathan Tracy became Grand Commander of the Grand Commandery, Knights Templar, of Texas.

Close Call

In July 1893, a young victim was rushed to Provident Hospital in Chicago with a near fatal stab wound. With the knife still embedded in the man's heart, hospital founder and Surgeon Daniel Hale Williams (1858-1931) performed the first known successful open-heart surgery in order to save the victim's life. Dr. Williams had a long list of medical accomplishments including service on the Illinois State Board of Health and a presidential appointment as Surgeon-in-Chief at Freedmen's Hospital in Washington, D.C. Named to the list of the 100 Greatest African Americans in 2001, Dr. Williams was a Prince Hall Freemason.

Dr. Williams' patient in that first successful open-heart surgery, James Cornish, lived for 50 years following the procedure.

Eighteen Minutes

The battle of the Alamo was a losing but inspirational part of the Texas war of independence. Heroic Freemasons William B. Travis, James Bowie, Davy Crockett and others lost their lives in the bloody fight, which lasted 12 grueling days. Forty-six days later at the Battle of San Jacinto, led by Brother Sam Houston, the Texans routed the Mexican army and won independence in a mere 18 minutes.

A Leaky Milk Wagon

Edward N. Hines, a member of Ashlar Lodge 91 in Detroit, was an innovator in the early development of highways. In 1909, he designed and built the first mile of paved road in the world, a stretch of Woodward Avenue between Six and Seven Mile roads in Detroit. In 1893 he published the first road tourbook and even in the infancy of their development started a movement for highway beautification. In 1911, a leaky milk wagon  he was following led him to develop one of the greatest highway safety features of all. The wagon was leaking a trail of white milk near the center of the road when Brother Hines got the idea for a white line to separate lanes, a standard feature on every highway in the world today.

The Great Zacchinni

When Freemason Paul Creason launched his career, he did it literally. Brother Creason was a GEN-U-INE human cannonball known as "Zacchinni" Creason. He is a member of Forsyth Lodge 453 in Missouri. Instead of working to support the Shrine Circus as many Brothers do, the Great Zacchinni has performed in it.

Brotherly Love Recommended

Boston's Old North Church, always associated with Brother Paul Revere's famous ride, was also the venue for the first known "Masonic sermon." On December 27, 1749, Brother Charles Brockwell delivered the message, "Brotherly Love Recommended" at the venerable site.

Jack The Ripper Hoax

Conspiracy theorists linking the Jack the Ripper killings to Freemasons (as depicted in the movie *From Hell*) overlook several important facts. First, many of those claimed to have been involved were not Freemasons. Second, Joseph Sickert, who originated the story, finally admitted it was a hoax in a comprehensive *Times of London* article. Also, Brother William Gull, alleged to have been the killer, was 72 years old and in poor health at the time of the crimes. Brother Gull had suffered a series of strokes and a heart attack prior to the time the killings started, and he would have been physically unable to commit the gruesome murders. In reality, Brother Gull was a standout physician who, among many

other well-known accomplishments, is credited with saving the life of the Price of Wales with one of the first recorded uses of CPR.

The Curse

As he was being bound to the stake in preparation for his execution, legend has it that Jacques DeMolay, Last Grand Master of the Knights Templar, invoked a curse on his persecutors. He is said to have vowed that King Phillip of France and Pope Clement would join him at the throne of God within a year to account for their sins. Both Phillip and Clement died within a year after DeMolay's martyrdom.

Academic Without A Degree

Walter Williams, 33°, (1864-1935) member of Twilight Lodge 114, Columbia, Missouri, was President of the University of Missouri, 1931-35, and founder in 1908 of the famous Journalism School at that institution. He served as dean of the school of journalism as well as its professor of history. He was the first president of the American Association of Schools and Departments of Journalism. Brother Williams also authored many books on Missouri history and the history of journalism. Although he was esteemed as an educator with remarkable academic achievements, Brother Williams never received any academic degree.

A Blunt And Caustic Sense Of Humor

Prince Philip, husband of Queen Elizabeth II, has been a member of Navy Lodge 2612 since 1952. A man of many titles, he is known for a blunt and caustic sense of humor which has garnered criticism on occasion. A few examples:

Upon hearing he was about to attend an event where Madonna would sing, he asked, "Do we need ear plugs?"

Constantly at odds with the press, he confronted a reporter at a gala and asked why he was there. The reporter responded that he had been invited. Philip shot back, "Well you didn't have to come."

He once quipped, "If you see a man opening a car door for a woman, it means one of two things: it's either a new car or a new woman."

Among his charitable works, Prince Philip is patron of the British Heart Foundation.

Poor Man, Rich Man

Coming to the California gold rush late, Brother Alvin Hayward entered a partnership with four other miners and purchased a claim in 1853. The group worked the mine for four years after which his discouraged partners declared it worthless and abandoned Hayward. Completely destitute, Brother Hayward had no choice but to continue working the mine alone. He spent a grueling year continuing to work the mine when, in 1858, he struck a huge vein of gold. With that good fortune, Brother Haywood eventually became the richest man in the state and went on to become High Priest of Sutter Creek Chapter 11. He was so rich he presented the Chapter with a golden altar and solid gold jewels of office.

Fort Masonic

At the height of the War of 1812, as the British closed in on New York, DeWitt Clinton, Grand Master of the Grand Lodge of New York, called Masons together to redoubt Fort Greene in what is now Brooklyn. The Brothers completed the work in a single day and then continued to support the stronghold, which came to be known as Fort Masonic. Because of the fort's existence, the British army skirted New York City and suffered a major defeat when it attacked Plattsburgh a month later. Doubtless, Fort Masonic and the Freemasons who fortified it contributed to saving the area from a fierce battle.

The Real Brothers Who "Invented" Flight

The brothers who "invented" flight were not the Wright Brothers. They were Jacques Etienne and Joseph Michel Montgolfier, both members of the famed Lodge of the Nine Sisters in Paris. Always fascinated by flight, Joseph had an epiphany one evening watching smoke rise from a fire and immediately fashioned a model hot air balloon. Based on the model, the brothers built a functioning full sized balloon which, after several experiments, they degor
trated before King Louis XVI and Marie Antoinette, with a sheep, rooster and duck on board. Upon seeing the demonstration the king declared the Montgolfier family to be royalty. Their invention carried the first human in free flight on November 21, 1783.

Large Jurisdiction

When the Grand Lodge of Missouri chartered Multnomah Lodge 84 in Oregon October 19, 1846, the Lodge's jurisdiction ran from the Canadian border on the north to the Mexican border on the south and from the Pacific Ocean to the Rocky mountains. At the same time, the jurisdiction of the Grand Lodge of Missouri covered all the territory between the Mississippi River to the Pacific.

Versatile Building

William R. MacVean of Middleton, NY as a boy in Glasgow, Scotland attended Sunday school, church and school in the same building. It was also the building where he was initiated, passed and raised as a Freemason. The building later served as a school for disabled children and today the building is the home of a school specializing in the education and care of autistic children.

From Non-Member To Shriner In Two Days

In a time when the Shrine required Rite membership and prior to the advent of 1-day classes it sometimes took quite a while to become a Mason and then proceed to the appendant bodies. In 1945, the Grand Master of Kansas granted special dispensation to an American hero to receive the degrees in less than the required time. General Jonathan M. Wainwright had been awarded the Congressional Medal of honor as the hero of Bataan in the WWII Pacific battle, was a prisoner of war for 39 months and had distinguished himself in the WWII European campaign. To accommodate his schedule, Brother Wainwright was initiated, passed and raised May 16, 1946, in Union Lodge 7, Junction City, Kansas. The following day, he took the Scottish Rite and Shrine degrees, going from a non-member to a Shriner in two days, a record at that time.

A Unique Hobby

King Gustaf V (1858-1950) was the longest reigning monarch of Sweden in spite of taking the throne at the relatively advanced age of 49. He ruled the country for 42 years, living to the age of 92, even though he was a heavy smoker. He served as Sweden's Grand Master and had the unique hobby of embroidery, using his skill to make altar cloths for churches.

A Terrible Mistake

Dr. Dodd compiling his "Thoughts in Prison."
DR. WILLIAM DODD,
EXECUTED FOR FORGERY

William Dodd was a man of God and good works who made a terrible mistake. Dodd, a Freemason, was also a poet and an author of commentaries on the Bible and Shakespeare. He served for a time as chaplain to the King of England, opened a facility to help reformed prostitutes change their lives and became one of the most popular preachers of his day. He lived extravagantly, acquired debts and in an impulsive move to pay them, forged a bond to obtain a loan. He was caught and convicted. Despite a popular movement to pardon him backed by a petition with 23,000 signatures, his conviction and sentence stood. At that time in England his offense was a capital crime and on June 27, 1777 he became the last person in England to be hanged for forgery.

Bare Facts

After visiting the Soviet Union Brother Will Rogers wrote a book entitled, *There's Not A Bathing Suit In Russia, And Other Bare Facts*. The publisher declined to put the second part of the title, suggestive by the standards of the day, on the book's cover.

The Gatterburg House

The Gatterburg House, home to the Grand Lodge of Austria, has been in continuous use as a Masonic building since the 18th century. Franz Joseph Haydn, the composer known as the "Father of the Symphony" was a member of Zur Wahren Eintrach ("True Concord") Lodge here, and Wolfgang Amadeus Mozart was a frequent visitor. Ignaz von Born, the leading scientist in the Holy Roman Empire, Master of the Lodge, lived and died in the building.

Peace And Harmony Not Prevailing

Leading forces against a Mexican uprising, Commander Nicolas Bravo, head of the Scottish Rite in Mexico, had General Vicente Guerrero, head of the York Rite, executed on February 17, 1831.

Brother Shakespeare?

William Shakespeare seems to have known something of Freemasonry:

"Whence come you?" (*Merry Wives of Windsor*, Act 4, Scene 5)

"Let's part on the word." (*Love's Labor Lost*, Act 4, Scene 2)

"Guard the door without. Let him not pass." (*Othello*, Act 5, Scene 2)

"The singing Masons building roofs of gold." (*Henry V*, Act 1, Scene 4)

"You made good work, you and your apron men." (*Cariolanus*, Act 4, Scene 6)

"Where is thy leathern apron and thy rule?" (*Julius Caesar*, Act 1, Scene 1)

"I will, as 'twere a Brother of your Order." (*Measure for Measure*, Act 1, Scene 4)

"They never meet, but they do square." (*A Midsummer Night's Dream*, Act 2, Scene 1)

A Yukon Lodge

During his lifetime, Andrew Carnegie funded libraries across the globe. In 1904, he commissioned construction of a library in Dawson City, Yukon Territories, Canada. Specifications called for the building to be made of stone, but that was not possible since  the ground fluctuated so much due to the area's permafrost. Instead, the town erected a wood frame building clad with metal and painted it to look as if it was a stone structure. A few years later, a fire gutted the building. The Freemasons in the area purchased the damaged structure, restored it to its original condition and today use it as their Lodge building.

King C. Gillette

 King C. Gillette (1855-1932), Columbian Lodge, Boston, was the inventor of the iconic razor bearing his name. Founder of the Gillette corporation, he built one of the great companies of the 20th century and is considered a pioneer titan of industry in the American capitalistic system. In spite of that, Brother Gillette was a committed Socialist.

Ironically, Gillette founded his company for the sole purpose of financing the promotion of a new Socialist system.

I Don't Believe In Ghosts, But...

Stories of haunted Masonic Lodges are as common as green beans at a Masonic dinner. The magnificent St. Louis Masonic Temple is not immune from its share of ghostly legends. Temple historian John Vollmann says he is a non-believer in such events, but while conducting a tour, shared the following: "I was working alone in the building. It was about 1AM and I suddenly heard a screeching sound. It stopped and I went back to work, but then I heard it again. I searched for the origin, but couldn't find it. When I went back to work the sound came back. So I turned up a radio, but couldn't drown out the sound. I don't believe in that kind of thing, but that's when I decided it would be a good time to leave the building."

Brother Guillotin, Dr. Guillotin And The Guillotine

Brother Joseph-Ignace Guillotin (1728-1814), a French physician, was a founding member of the Grand Orient of France, a member of the famed Lodge of the Nine Sisters in Paris and Master of Concorde Fraternelle Lodge in 1719. He also founded the French Academy of Medicine. Legend has it he invented the guillotine and was eventually executed by the device. Neither is true. Brother Guillotin did, however, suggest death for the condemned should be as speedy and painless as possible, leading to the machine's invention and name. By coincidence another doctor, J.M.V. Guillotin from Lyons, met his death by guillotine and the similarity of name and profession led to the confusion with Brother Guillotin, who died of natural causes at home in Paris.

Received Of Stephen F. Austin...

Receipt for Stephen Austin's initiation fee and dues to Louisiana Lodge 109 (Ste. Genevieve, Missouri): "Received of Stephen F. Austin Twenty Dollars for his Initiation fees, as [and] also Seventy five Cents for Dues to Louisiana Lodge no. 109, in full of all his dues up to this date. Ste. Genevieve June 26th, 1815. Signed by Theodore F. Long, Treas." In today's dollars, that calculates to an initiation fee of approximately $240 and dues of $9, but the receipt does not indicate if the dues amount is for a full year.

Masonic Meeting In The Senate Chambers

Senator Henry Clay, Past Grand Master of Kentucky, was instrumental in setting up a meeting held in Washington, DC, on March 9, 1822. The meeting resulted in a resolution to establish a General Grand Lodge. Although that body was never formed, the meeting itself is significant in that it is the only Masonic meeting on record ever held in the United States Senate chambers.

Panty Raid

A Grand Lodge of California account from the mid-1960s describes a crime in which a Brother had been convicted of the theft of clothing, including 181 pairs of women's undergarments. The official police report described the incident as a "panty raid," stemming from the popular (and self-explanatory) hi-jinx occurring on college campuses at the time. The Brother came up on Masonic charges. In order to distinguish his serious crime from some youthful indiscretion, the Grand Lodge of California Proceedings for that year included the following: "We do not wish to be misunderstood as overemphasizing the gravity of that specification against the accused in which he is charged with a 'panty raid.' Indulgence in such conduct by boys of college age for the purpose of displaying either skill or courage, if that be the purpose, differs from the conduct of the accused here, in that the theft of 181 pairs of ladies pants is not merely a playful prank."

Sin-Suffer-Repent

Brother Henry Lieferant (1892-1968), Lodge unknown, was a Polish-born and educated immigrant to the US who became a prolific author with several books and magazine articles to his credit. As Editor-in-chief of True Story magazine, he was responsible for is rise to popularity when he developed the story format whereby a heroine "violates standards of behavior, suffers as a consequence, learns her lesson and resolves to live in light of it, unembittered by her pain." True Story magazine still survives using Brother Lieferant's tried-and-true, if not slightly salacious format known as "sin-suffer-repent."

Grand Master Of Masons Of The US

January 13, 1780 the Grand Lodge of Pennsylvania proposed unifying Freemasonry in the country and elected George Washington as the first Grand Master of Masons of the United States. When the Grand Lodge of Massachusetts failed to act on the matter, the issue faded away and Washington never assumed the office.

A Steam Powered Typewriter

Worshipful Brother Theodore F. Randolph (1816-1883), Varick Lodge 31, Jersey City, served both as Governor and Senator from New Jersey. Prior to entering politics, WB Randolph was an industrialist, entrepreneur and inventor. Among his inventions were a stitching machine and a steam powered typewriter. Not surprisingly, the steam typewriter did not catch on.

His Luck Ran Out

Brother Earl "Lucky" Teter was an American stunt driver in the 1930s and 1940s who was the first to use the label "Hell Drivers." A member of Noblesville Lodge 57 in Indiana, Teter left his job as a pump jockey to form his stunt driving team, which barnstormed the country with its repertoire of automobile thrills and spills. On July 4, 1942, 41 year old Teter announced it was his last show prior to closing for the war effort. He made 3 jumps over a panel truck that day, each attempting a world record, beginning at 135 feet. His 4th and final jump was 150 feet and was dedicated "to all servicemen everywhere." Some reported they could hear the engine missing in his bright yellow 1938 Plymouth as he accelerated onto the launching ramp. Teter's luck ran out as his jump fell short and he lost his life.

Royal Arch Gunnison

On June 24, 1873, Brother Christopher B. Gunnison attended a York Rite Chapter meeting. He returned home to find his pregnant wife had given birth unexpectedly. Since the baby was born while Christopher was at a Chapter Meeting, he suggested naming him "Royal Arch." Royal Arch Gunnison (1873-1918) grew up to become a federal judge in Alaska and, yes, a Royal Arch Mason.

Royal Arch Gunnison

Frank Land: Artist

The world came to know Frank Land as a man who created a premiere youth organization, who had superb administrative skills and one who was a friend of presidents and diplomats. Few realized he was also an accomplished artist who even used some of his own artwork for the organization he created. One of his earliest surviving works depicts a young woman kneeling at prayer and is almost reminiscent of a DeMolay scene. This 1909 pen and ink drawing hangs today in the Kansas City Service and Leadership Center.

He Refused To Dine On A Co-Star

Brother Will Rogers, Claremore Lodge 53, Claremore, Oklahoma, once refused to eat a co-star. In the 1933 movie *State Fair*, Rogers worked with "Blue Boy," a champion hog. Blue Boy was so temperamental during the filming that Director Henry King gave him to Rogers to slaughter and eat. Brother Rogers instead donated Blue Boy to an agricultural college.

Ecuador Hats?

Eloy Alfaro was an Ecuadorian liberator and President of the country from 1906-11. His Lodge is unknown, but his Masonic status is not in doubt: his anti-Masonic successor as President had him imprisoned and ultimately killed for being a Freemason! Following

his presidential term, Brother Alfaro lived in Panama in exile. While there, he imported toquilla hats from Ecuador and sold them to finance his revolution. The hats were immensely popular and since they came from Panama, were assumed to have originated there. Named to reflect that fact, "Panama hats" were introduced to the world by Brother Eloy Alfaro, and they actually come from Ecuador.

The Woz

Steve Wozniak, co-founder of Apple Computer, is a life member of Charity Lodge 362 in Campbell, California. He joined the fraternity at the urging of his wife, Alice. Alice thought the strong moral and spiritual values of the Masons would help improve their failing relationship, and allow them to spend more time together since she was an active member of the Eastern Star. Masonic values may not falter, but unfortunately, marriages do. Their marriage failed shortly after "The Woz" was raised in 1980.

He Stayed At His Post

Among the many stories of valor at Pearl Harbor was the heroism of Brother Jesse D. Jewell. Brother Jewell, St. Paul's Lodge 14, Newport, RI, was a physician stationed aboard the USS California. Severely burned about the face and arms, he stayed at his post and administered medical care to the wounded men on his ship. Credited with saving many lives on that day, he was cited for his courage, determination and devotion and awarded the coveted Navy Cross.

Fluent In Ten Languages

Samuel Hahnemann (1755-1843) was a member of Lodge Minerva in Leipzig, Germany. He founded homeopathy, a branch of medicine based on the principle that a disease could be cured by drugs that would produce symptoms of itself in a healthy person. Brother Hahnemann's research led him to study and translate texts in several languages. Over the course of his lifetime in addition to his native language of German, he became fluent in English, French, Italian, Greek, Latin, Arabic, Syriac, Chaldaic and Hebrew.

World's Smallest Mason

Three men laid claim to being the world's smallest Mason: Charles Stratton (1838-1883) at 40" and 70 pounds, St. John's Lodge 3, Bridgeport, Connecticut; Vance Swift (1916-1946) at 26" and 34 pounds, Pythagoras Lodge 355, New Albany, Indiana; and Reuben Steere (1838-1904) at 44" and 43 pounds, Friendship Lodge 7, Chepachet, Rhode Island. The distinction seems to go to Brother Swift, who also claimed to be the world's smallest man. Stratton, raised in 1862, was the shortest Mason of his time and by far the most famous of the three, better known by another name, "Tom Thumb."

Tom Thumb

Brougham

The term "Brougham" has been used by every single American car manufacturer as well as a few foreign ones to designate a car model or trim package with richly appointed features. It refers to the elegant "Brougham" carriage popular in the 19th century. That carriage was originally built to the specifications of and named for Lord Henry Peter Brougham, 1st Baron Brougham and Vaux, a British statesman who became Lord Chancellor of Great Britain. Brother Brougham was a member of Canongate Kilwinning Lodge 2 of Edinburgh Scotland.

A Role He Could Sink His Teeth Into

Glenn Ford, a member of Riviera Lodge 780 in Pacific Palisades, California, got his big break when Humphrey Bogart turned down the role of Johnny Farrell in the 1946 blockbuster, *Gilda*. In one scene his co-star, Rita Hayworth, repeatedly and violently struck Brother Ford's character. During one of the takes she hit him with a blow so hard it knocked a tooth out. Ford waited until after the scene was over to tell anyone he had been injured.

Martha Washington's Courageous Act

Martha Washington was terrified of battlefields, yet she spent fully half of the American Revolution with her husband George, a courageous act that has been largely lost to history.

Gambling Class

Virgil and Wyatt Earp

Famous frontier Marshals Virgil and Wyatt Earp were not always on the right side of the law. At various times each was involved in gambling and prostitution and they were heavily criticized for their handling of the events leading up to the "Gunfight at the OK Corral" and its aftermath. Prior to the famed gunfight in 1881, Virgil attempted to join the

Freemasons at Solomon Lodge (UD) in Tombstone. The investigating committee reported favorably but the lodge rejected his petition, the members feeling Virgil was a member of the "gambling class."

Lodge Fines

The 1765 bylaws of Joppa Lodge 1, Maryland, state, "Any Brother who shall misbehave himself in Lodge, either by unbecoming language, cursing, speaking obscenely or apparently intoxicated with liquor shall pay a fine of two shillings and sixpence for each such offense." Adjusting for inflation and currency changes, this amounts to about five of today's US dollars.

The Masonic Sign

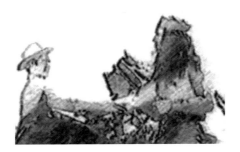

Traveling west of Laramie, Wyoming in 1874, members of a wagon train became concerned when a band of Native American Indians began following them. A Freemason traveling with the group, known only as Brother Reid, had heard there were Masons among the tribes, so he rode off to meet their pursuers. Approaching the Indians, Brother Reid identified himself as a Freemason and gave a Masonic sign. After a brief conversation, the Indians turned, rode away and never bothered the wagon train again, with Brother Reid giving the Masonic sign credit for saving the wagon train.

Unique Bonds Of Friendship

The Friend to Friend Masonic Memorial in the Gettysburg National Cemetery depicts a scene where the fatally wounded Confederate General Lewis Armistead entrusts his personal effects to Union Captain Henry H. Bingham, knowing him to be a Brother Freemason. The memorial, a gift from the Grand Lodge of Pennsylvania, is dedicated to the Freemasons of the Civil War, "Their unique bonds of friendship enabled them to remain a brotherhood undivided..."

Border Lodges

Golden Rule Lodge 5, Stanstead, Quebec was originally located on the border between Quebec and Vermont, with the Canadian/US border splitting the Lodge room. Similarly, today, the International Peace Garden Lodge of Freemasons is situated in a square and compasses shaped building near the border between Manitoba and North Dakota, located north of Dunseith, North Dakota. The Lodge was formed in 1993, with Warrants granted by the Grand Lodges of Manitoba, North Dakota and Minnesota. The Grand Lodge of Saskatchewan became a chartering Grand Lodge in 2000. Membership in the International Peace Garden Lodge of Freemasons is open to any Master Mason in good standing for a once-in-a-lifetime fee of $50.00.

Had He Been Elected...

Wendell L. Willkie (1892-1944), Quincy Lodge 230, Elwood, Indiana, was the Republican nominee for President of the United States in 1940, running against Brother Franklin D. Roosevelt. All things equal, had Brother Willkie been elected, he would have died in office October 8, 1944.

First Honorary Citizen Of The US

Sir Winston Churchill, Rosemary Lodge 2581, London, British Prime Minister and one of the great leaders of the 20th century, on April 9, 1963, became the first person ever to receive the designation "Honorary Citizen of the United States."

Only 7 people hold this rare distinction. Among them are Marquis de Lafayette, A Freemason who is also an Honorary member of the Grand Lodge of Missouri and Casimir Pulaski, reported to be a member of Gould Lodge of Georgia. Congress granted 5 of the honorary citizenships posthumously, with Brother Churchill and Mother Theresa being the only designates to receive the honor while living.

Joseph Warren's Dental Crown

Joseph Warren, physician and American Revolution Major General was a member of Lodge of St. Andrew, Boston. While still Grand Master in Massachusetts, he died fighting at the Battle of Bunker Hill. His body was buried near the area where he died and remained there for 10 months until friends and family made an effort to find it. Searchers would never have identified his remains were it not for a silver dental crown Brother Warren had. The crown was crafted and given to him by his good friend, American patriot and master silversmith, Brother Paul Revere.

Class Action

Josiah Quincy (1772-1864), St. John's Lodge of Boston, was Harvard's 15th president, serving from 1829-1845. In 1834, an argument between a student and teacher escalated and resulted in disciplinary action against several students. The disciplined students' classmates rioted after the action, breaking windows and furniture and otherwise disrupting campus life. Things got so out-of-hand, Brother Quincy expelled the entire sophomore class.

The Iconic Bucking Horse

Lester C. Hunt, a member of Wyoming Lodge 2 in Lander, served as Governor and a US Senator from his state. He may be best remembered, however, for something he did as Wyoming's

Secretary of State. Serving in that position in 1936, he designed Wyoming's iconic "bucking horse" license plate, commissioning famed western landscape artist Allen T. True of Authors Lodge 3456 in London to complete the final artwork. Every quarter for the remainder of his life, Brother Hunt received a royalty of $3.50 from the state for the use of his design. Instead of cashing the checks, he endorsed them over to the state treasury.

Memphis

Memphis, Tennessee, founded in 1819, was named after Egypt's ancient Nile River capital. The town was originally to have been named Jackson, in honor of Most Worshipful Brother Andrew Jackson. Brother Jackson, however, declined to have the town so named. He got his due when 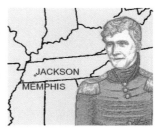 Alexandria, a settlement on the Forked Deer River in central western Tennessee was named for him three years later. The town so honored Jackson primarily because of his successes as a general, seven years before he became President of the US.

The Royal Arch House

The 1832 election pitted Brother Andrew Jackson against Anti-Masonic Party candidate William Wirt. Paul Boynton, a dedicated Freemason, declared if his state, Vermont, voted for Wirt, he would leave. As it would happen, Vermont was the only state Wirt took and, true to his  word, Brother Boynton moved to Canton, New York. There, to demonstrate his loyalty to the craft, he built "The Royal Arch House," where he lived for the remainder of his life. The building was replete with Masonic symbolism including a central room known as "The Third Veil" and a hidden secret chamber where Masonic Lodges in the area met throughout the peak of the anti-Masonic period.

Ecumenical Group

On May 31, 1801, Brother John Mitchell along with Fredrick Dalcho and nine others established the first Supreme Council of the Scottish Rites in America. Of those eleven men, four were Jewish, two were Roman Catholic and five were Protestants of various denominations.

Hoe Cakes

Brother George Washington's favorite breakfast was "hoe cakes." Similar to today's pancakes, they were so named because they could be fried on the back of a common garden tool, a flat hoe. The General preferred to eat his serving "liberally drizzled with butter and honey."

Dan Brown On Freemasonry

"In a world where men do battle over whose definition of God is most accurate, I cannot adequately express the deep respect and admiration I feel toward [the Freemasons], an organization in which men of differing faiths are able to 'break bread together' in a bond of brotherhood, friendship, and camaraderie."
~Dan Brown, author The Lost Symbol

Wooden Revolver

In 1832, his father sent him on a voyage to learn the seaman's trade. But Samuel Colt (1814-1862) was more interested in mechanical things, having grown up working in his father's factory. On the voyage, he observed the mechanics of the ship's wheel, discovering "regardless of which way the wheel was spun, each spoke always came in direct line with a clutch that could be set to hold it." The motion gave the eighteen-year-old an idea and the revolving pistol was born. Having  nothing else to work with on the ship, he built the world's first revolver out of wood, and went on to make a fortune as the founder of Colt's Patent Fire-Arms Manufacturing Company. Brother Colt was a member of St. John's Lodge 4, Hartford, Connecticut.

A Poem A Day For Forty Years

 American Poet Edgar Guest, Ashlar Lodge 91 of Detroit, was known as the "People's Poet." Unlike many poets who starve and wallow in obscurity, Brother Guest was labeled the "foremost poet of the 20th century," and made a very comfortable living with his works. He was so prolific, he penned over 15,000 poems by writing a poem a day for over 40 years!

President Harding's Last Speech

Brother Warren G. Harding's last speech was delivered after his death. Brother Harding had planned to make an address at a meeting of Hollywood Commandery 56, KT, on August 2, 1923, but died earlier that day. His private secretary, Sir Knight George B. Christian, Marion Lodge 70, Ohio, attended in his stead. In front of a somber and saddened gathering, Brother Christian gave the speech the President had planned to deliver.

Expensive Postage

Most Worshipful Brother John Marshall (1755 - 1835) was 4th Chief Justice of the US Supreme Court and two-term Grand Master of the Grand Lodge of Virginia (1793-1795). In August, 1895, the United States honored MWB Marshall by issuing his likeness on a $5 postage stamp. In today's currency, that amounts to a whopping $129. The stamp was so expensive there is no record of its use until March, 1896. Subsequently, the largest existing block of these stamps was discovered on a parcel containing containing 14 of them, amounting to over $1,800 in postage in today's dollars. In 1902, the Post Office redesigned the stamp, and in the fall of 2010, one of the stamps in mint condition sold for over $3,000.

Freemason And Mastermason

Twin sailing ships worked along the eastern seaboard of the Colonies/United States during the 18th century. One was named the *Freemason*, the other was the *Mastermason*. The origin of their names is unknown, but clearly, someone with a Masonic background commissioned them. The pair could be seen plying the shores from 1737 until 1779, when the *Freemason* caught fire and sank in Marblehead Harbor, Massachusetts.

The Epiphany

A victim of political and personal persecution, Charles L. Cadet-Gassincourt (1769-1821), blamed the Freemasons for his troubles and became a staunch anti-Mason. He published the book "The Fall of Jacques DeMolay," in which he claimed Freemasonry was the cause of all European political dysfunction. In his vehement detestation of Freemasonry he became obsessed with researching its failings. His prolific research into the Craft led him to a stunning conclusion: that his accusations against Freemasonry were untrue and it was a worthy and just fraternity. Having had this epiphany, he petitioned Lodge l'Abeille in Paris, and became its Master in 1805.

The George Washington Of Italy

Often called "The George Washington of Italy," Giuseppe Garibaldi fought for the independence of no less than three countries: Italy, Uruguay and Brazil. Somehow in the midst of all this, he found time to be Grand Commander of the Supreme Council, 33°, AASR, in Italy as well as Grand Master of Italy. In the US, he was affiliated with Tompkins Lodge 471 in Stapleton, New York.

Wards Of His Own School

Bartholomew Ruspini, a member of Burning Bush Lodge in Bristol, England and founding member of the Lodge of the Nine Muses, was a progressive 18th century dental surgeon who developed one of the earliest forms of toothpaste. He founded the Royal Masonic School for Girls, which still exists today. He used most of his resources for charity and when he died, left a modest annuity which could support only his wife — two of his granddaughters therefore becoming wards of the Royal Masonic School he had founded.

The Roosevelt Dime

The US Mint issued a dime carrying Franklin Roosevelt's portrait just nine months after his death. Known as the Roosevelt dime, it has been in continuous circulation since. The reverse side shows an olive branch symbolizing peace, a torch (the same one held by the Statue of Liberty) symbolizing freedom, and an oak branch which symbolizes safety, security and strength.

Lux in Tenebris

Lux in Tenebris 3856 is a London Lodge for blind Freemasons. Appropriately, the name of the Lodge means "Light in Darkness.

Home Sweet Home

Sir Henry Rowley Bishop, Lodge unknown, was an English composer most famous for writing the song *Home Sweet Home* (Be it ever so humble, there's no place like home). Queen Victoria knighted Brother Bishop in 1842, when he became the first musician ever to receive that honor.

Brother Nicholas' Recruiting Program

On November 5, 1775, the Second Continental Congress commissioned Samuel Nicholas "Captain of Marines" making him the first Marine officer and, by definition, the first Commandant of the Marine Corps. Brother Nicholas, Lodge 13, Philadelphia, faced a tough recruiting environment head-on by opening his office in the Tun Tavern and provisioning the corps with sharp uniforms of red, white, black, and green that appealed not only to the young recruits but, possibly more importantly, to young ladies.

Ouch!

George Rogers Clark (1752-1818) was the highest ranking military officer on the western frontier in the American Revolution. He was also the brother of famed Freemason William Clark (of the Lewis and Clark expedition). A Freemason, George Rogers Clark's Lodge is unknown, but Abraham Lodge 8, Louisville conducted his Masonic funeral. In 1809, at age 57, Brother Clark suffered a stroke and fell into a fireplace, burning his leg so badly it required amputation. When Dr. Richard Ferguson, Master of Abraham Lodge, performed the amputation, the only anesthetic Brother Clark received was music from a fife and drum corps playing in the background.

A Diminutive Man With An Enormous Nose

Andrew Bell, primary founder of Encyclopedia Britannica, Holyrood House Lodge 44 of Edinburgh Scotland, was a diminutive man who stood only 4 foot 6 inches tall. Despite his small stature, the proud Bell always rode the tallest horse he could get. He mounted and dismounted his horse using a ladder, many times to the cheers of onlookers. His features included an enormous nose which occasionally drew stares. Brother Bell fashioned an even larger paper mache nose, which he could affix over his already large beak and when he caught people gawking, he would put the fake nose on and gawk back giving them the graphic message that it's not polite to stare.

The Steamboat

John Fitch (1743-1798), Bristol Lodge 25, Pennsylvania, invented the steamboat, first putting a prototype into operation in 1787. Discouraged after years of unsuccessfully trying to obtain funding to commercialize his invention, Brother Fitch poisoned himself, leaving a suicide note which said, "The day will come when some more powerful man will get fame and riches from my invention; but nobody will believe that poor John Fitch can do anything worthy of attention." That man was Robert Fulton, whom most people today credit with the steamboat's invention.

The Funeral Omnibus

George Shillibeer, Globe Lodge 23 of London, had a successful carriage business, specializing in the manufacture of elegant hearses. He invented a way to make carriages longer and larger than ever before and manufactured those, calling his huge vehicle an "omnibus." With that, he established London's omnibus system, a forerunner of the bus system running there today. Given his successes with those two types of vehicles, he also invented a carriage which combined a hearse and a bus. The public's cool reception and short life of Brother Shillibeer's "Funeral Omnibus" confirms that not all ideas are good ones.

Five-Pointed Stars

Little is known about Betsy Ross (1752-1836). History reveals she probably did not make the first flag, but was one of many seamstresses working on the project. She had three husbands and three graves. First buried in a Quaker cemetery, her body was moved to a public cemetery in 1856. In 1976, moving her remains for burial at her home for the Bicentennial, workers found no bones and speculated which bones in the family plot were hers. Her "grave" is now at her home but it is uncertain if the remains are hers. What is certain is that stars on the original flag were to have six points, but Betsy Ross devised a way to make five-pointed stars with a single cut from fabric folded just right. Were it not for her, today's flags would have six-pointed stars. At the time she worked on the flag project, she was married to Brother John Claypoole and to the degree that myth matches reality, it may well be the first American flag was made in the home of a Freemason.

Feared Lost

In September, 2001, St. John's Lodge 1 in New York loaned the precious Washington inaugural Bible to the Fraunces Tavern Museum for display. Located just a few blocks from the World Trade Center, the attacks of September 11 blanketed the area with dust, debris and rubble. Authorities cordoned off the area and the Brothers feared the priceless relic may have been damaged or lost. Two days later, Brother Tom Savini, Director of the Livingston Masonic Library, obtained a special escort to the Fraunces Tavern Museum, where he found the Washington Bible intact and unharmed.

John Paul Jones' Missing Body

The body of Brother John Paul Jones, "Father of the American Navy" was lost for 113 years. Brother Jones died a lonely and forgotten man in Paris in 1792. A friend paid for a lead coffin and Jones was buried in the Protestant cemetery. Appointed ambassador to France in 1899, General Horace Porter became obsessed with finding Brother Jones' remains. He found them, well-preserved thanks to the lead coffin, after a six year search. The US government transported the American hero's remains home Where President and Masonic Brother Theodore Roosevelt presided over a grand funeral. Eventually Jones' remains were placed in an elaborate sarcophagus at the United States Naval Academy in Annapolis.

Gormogons

In 18th century England, a pseudo-secret society, the Gormogons, required prospective members to mock Freemasons prior to being admitted as members.

Lodge Of The Arts

Brother William Paley

St. Cecile Lodge 568, New York, "The Lodge of the Arts," boasts a membership consisting of world famous artists, past and present. Among its membership are Brothers William Paley, Paul Whiteman, Al Jolson, Harry Houdini, Bert Williams, D. W. Griffith, Louis B. Mayer, Vincent Lopez, Otto Kruger and others, too many to name.

The Nuclear Trigger

After World War II, the United States began an atomic weapons testing program at Eniwetok Atoll in the South Pacific. Major General John E. Hull (a member of Oxford Lodge 67 in Ohio) commanded the operation. On the morning of April 14, 1948 Brother Hull figuratively became the first person to pull the trigger on a nuclear device during peacetime when the US detonated the first atomic bomb there.

Freedom Fighters

Miguel Hidalgo y Costilla, Arquitechtura Moral Lodge of Mexico City, and Francisco I. Madero, Lealtad Lodge 15 of Mexico City, led Mexican revolutions exactly a century apart. Both, considered heroes and freedom fighters, were jointly honored when Mexico issued a silver ten-peso coin in 1960, bearing their likenesses. Brother Madero became President of Mexico for a short time but was overthrown in a counter-revolution. He was captured and executed in 1913 while "attempting to escape." Brother Hidalgo faced a firing squad in 1811. The government beheaded his body after his execution, impaled his head on a stake and, as a warning to other insurgents, left it on public display for ten years.

Don Benito

Benjamin Davis Wilson, Los Angeles Lodge 42 and Pentalphia Lodge 202, was a California statesman who became the second Mayor of Los Angeles. Mount Wilson and the famed observatory that sits atop it were named in his honor. At a time of acts of unspeakable violence toward them, Native Americans called him Don Benito because of his benevolence toward  the tribes in his area. Brother Wilson is also the grandfather of World War II General George S. Patton, Jr., a man not known for benevolence toward anyone.

Sacramento Chapter 3

 A single California Chapter of Royal Arch Masons, Sacramento Chapter 3, has been the home Chapter for no less than four California Governors: John Neely Johnson (1825-1872), Milton S. Latham (1827-1882), Romualdo Pacheco (1831-1899) and Hiram W. Johnson (1866-1945).

An Adventurous Life

Top WWI flying ace, recipient of the Distinguished Service Cross and Congressional Medal of Honor winner, Edward V. "Eddie" Rickenbacker (1890-1973) led one of the most adventurous lives of any 20th century American. Left for dead in a horrific 1941 airliner crash, he survived only to be lost at sea and adrift in a raft for three weeks the

following year, while on a presidential mission. A man of many talents, Rickenbacker was an air racer, drove in four Indianapolis 500-mile races and then purchased and ran the Indianapolis Motor Speedway. He also developed 4-wheel braking for cars, ran Eastern Airlines and even scripted the "Ace Drummond" comic strip. Brother Eddie Rickenbacker, 33°, was a member of Kilwinning Lodge 297, Detroit, Michigan, Moslem Shrine Temple and Detroit York Rite Bodies.

Exaggerated

Brother Mark Twain did not exactly say, "The reports of my death are greatly exaggerated." What he did say, in this note to family, was, "James Ross Clemens, a cousin of mine was seriously ill two or three weeks ago in London, but is well now. The report of my illness grew out of his illness, the report of my death was an exaggeration." Years later, Twain had no problem when people attributed the more famous phrase to him.

Astronomical Recognition

Brother John Wallis, Lodge unknown, was an English mathematician who was a co-developer of infinitesimal calculus. He was one of the founders of England's Royal Society, a renowned group still in existence which supports scientific achievement and advancement. He served as the chief cryptographer for Parliament (1643-1689) and a member of the Royal Court. He also introduced the modern symbol for infinity: ∞. Overshadowed by some of his peers in the founding of the Royal Society and the development of calculus (e.g., Isaac Newton), he has remained largely forgotten. However, in 2000, he was recognized for his accomplishments when astronomers named a newly discovered main-belt asteroid "31982 Johnwallis."

The Bazooka

Brother Bob "Bazooka" Burns (1890-1956), WWII era comedian invented a wacky horn he used in his act and called it a "Bazooka." The horn was shaped like a tube with a flared end. The WWII shoulder fired anti-tank rocket launcher had a similar shape and was nicknamed the "Bazooka" after Brother Bob's contraption.

Independence Hall

Independence Hall in Philadelphia stands on ground purchased by William Allen, Grand Master of Pennsylvania. Brother Edmund Woolley staked out the building position. Brother Benjamin Franklin laid the cornerstone in 1734, when he was Grand Master and was assisted by St. John's Lodge. Brother Andrew McNair rang the bell to summon citizens on July 8,
1776 to hear the reading of the Declaration of Independence, and the Liberty Bell cracked while tolling the Death of Chief Justice John Marshall, Past Grand Master of Virginia.

Exiled Three Times

Brother Charles Louis Napoleon Bonaparte — Napoleon III (1808-1873) was both the first elected president of France and its last reigning monarch. A tumultuous autocrat, he was exiled three times, escaped after being sentenced to life in prison and on other occasions welcomed as a hero. A member of the Ancient and Accepted Scottish Rite of France, the national assembly finally deposed him in 1871, when he retired with his family to England.

Largest Master's Chair

Ophir Lodge 33, Murphys, California, has the largest known Master's chair, measuring 15 feet long. The chair seats the Master, Past Master and all visiting dignitaries. In use for decades, Ophir now keeps the chair in its upstairs "Museum Lodge" and uses it on special occasions and when performing degree work for other Lodges.

Clerks of Relaxed Observance

In 1767, Johann August von Starck established a Masonic Order for Knights Templar, which he called Clerks of Relaxed Observance. As its name implies, it was formed as an antithetical body to Strict Observance Lodges, but later merged with them. The order consisted of seven degrees which embodied the idea that Templarism was a hierarchy within which every Mason was a Templar and every Templar was a Knight and a Priest. In order to join the Clerks of Relaxed Observance, a Brother first had to be a member of the Roman Catholic Church.

Butterfield's Lullaby

Medal of Honor recipient Daniel Adams Butterfield was a Union General in the Civil war and a member of Metropolitan Lodge 373 in New York. Stationed at Harrison's Landing in July, 1862, Brother Butterfield composed a few new bugle calls for his troops. One in particular was a haunting tune which became known as "Butterfield's Lullaby." General Butterfield, used it to replace the customary firing of three rifle volleys at the end of burials during battle. He also had the tune played to signal the end of the day's activities. The tune caught on and within months both Union and Confederate troops were using it as the bugle call at day's end. The military continues that tradition to this day, now simply calling "Butterfield's Lullaby" by its more common name, "Taps."

He Who Takes Long Strides

Brother John Rae (1813-1893) was a Scottish explorer of the Arctic recognized for his endurance. He is known to have hiked over 23,000 miles on snowshoes in his lifetime. He covered great distances by limiting supplies and living with and in the manner of Eskimos. Owing to his ability to cover such distances in adverse conditions, his Intuit name was Aglooka, "he who takes long strides." He certainly lived up to it, once accomplishing the amazing feat of traveling 100 miles on snowshoes in a single day.

The Psychiatrist And The Sea Scouts

Dr. William C. Menninger in 1924 became a Freemason in New York City while still an intern at Bellvue Hospital. He co-founded the world renowned Menninger clinic in Topeka, Kansas. He was medical director of the clinic for 16 years and, along with his brother Karl (Topeka Lodge 17), received world wide recognition in the field of psychiatry. Amazingly, this psychiatric icon from landlocked Topeka, Kansas, was also the original author of the Sea Scouts Skipper's Handbook.

Shoes For The Inaugural Ball

John E. Osborne, a member of Sisco Lodge 259 in Westport, New York, was Wyoming's third governor and the first Democrat to occupy that office. After a mob lynched the notorious outlaw George "Big Nose" Parrott in 1881, Brother Osborne, also a physician, took possession of the body to perform an autopsy. Completing that,

Brother Osborne sent Parrott's skin to a tannery, where it was made into a pair of shoes. Subsequently, in 1883, having been elected governor, Osborne wore those shoes to his inaugural ball.

Masonic Funerals

Bother William Brockmeier (1866-1947) of St. Louis, Missouri, conducted 5,586 Masonic Funerals over the course of his Masonic life. During the time he was actively presiding at funerals, this would have amounted to an average of 2-3 funerals per week over a period of 40 years.

The Grand Honors

Baron Johann de Kalb (most likely a member of Army Lodge 29 of Pennsylvania) lost his life rallying his American troops during the Revolutionary War Battle of Camden. The opposing commander, Lord Charles Cornwallis personally tended to his mortally wounded Brother, who had been shot 11 times. Then, when Brother de Kalb died, Brother Cornwallis performed the grand honors of Masonry at his funeral.

The Greatest Leader

Ernest Shackleton, a member of Wooster Lodge 79 and Siloam Lodge 32 in Connecticut, was a pioneer Antarctic explorer. During an expedition in January, 1915, Shackleton's ship "Endurance" became locked in an ice floe. Eventually the pressure of the ice crushed the ship's hull, rendering it useless except for shelter and provisions.

Shackleton and his crew set up camp on the huge chunk of ice as it wandered aimlessly in the sea until April 14, 1916, when the men spotted land and rowed their lifeboats to the safety of Antarctica's Elephant Island. All had survived after nearly 16 months of isolation. Shackleton's ability to maintain calm, ration supplies and care for the men during the ordeal led one reporter to call him, "the greatest leader that ever came upon God's earth, bar none."

Nine Day Wonder

Upon his election as Governor of New Hampshire, Joseph A. Gilmore became a "Mason at Sight" April 28, 1863. He received the 33° AASR (Northern Jurisdiction) on May 7, 1863, just nine days later!

Washington On The Side Of The British?

Young George Washington

As a teenager, Brother George Washington joined the British Navy. His mother had recently lost her husband and had another son serving as a British seaman, a dangerous profession at best. She begged young George to change his mind until he finally relented and resigned. Had Brother Washington ignored his mother's pleas, the man who became General of the Armies in the American Revolution, the first President and the Father of His Country would have fought for the other side!

The Rest Is History

St. John's Lodge 1 in New York has the honor of having the Bible upon which George Washington took his presidential oath of office. It wasn't planned that way but when Brother Washington was preparing to take the oath, someone noticed there was no Bible to be  found. Aids went in search of one and seeing St. John's Lodge (at the time Lodge number 2) across the street they knew it would have a Bible. They rushed in, borrowed it and, as they say, the rest is history.

Alexander M. Dockery

 Alexander M. Dockery, Jackson Lodge 82, Linneus, Missouri, served as Governor of Missouri, Grand Master of Missouri, Grand High Priest of the Grand Chapter, R.A.M., of Missouri and Grand Master of Odd Fellows in Missouri.

Edwin Booth And Robert Lincoln

Brother Edwin Booth, the most famous actor of his time and a member of New York Lodge 330, heroically saved a young man from being crushed by a train during the Civil War. Booth's courageous act was made more notable by the fact that the young man was Robert Lincoln, son of  President Lincoln. In an even more incredible twist, Edwin Booth was the brother of Lincoln's assassin, John Wilkes Booth.

Oldest Scottish Rite Document

The Reverend Frederick Dalcho, first Lt. Grand Commander of the Scottish Rite, was a Charleston, South Carolina, physician who also became an Episcopal priest and edited the Charleston Courier. He maintained Freemasonry dated back to the very creation of the world. Dalcho received his thirty-third degree May 25, 1801. His patent is the oldest Scottish Rite document in existence.

The Goose And Gridiron

The ancient society of the Swan and Lyre, dating back to 1500, described itself as a "Worshipful company of Musicians," and was an effort of organize London minstrels into a guild. It used as its symbol a swan standing on a crest beneath a lyre and ultimately met at a local tavern. In the 18th century the tavern owners, in a not-so-veiled attempt to mock the pretentious name of the society, designed a crest with a goose standing in front of a griddle, and named the tavern the Goose and Gridiron. There, on June 24, 1717, four Lodges met to form what has become modern Freemasonry.

Truman's SOTU

Harry Truman's 1947 State of the Union address was the first one shown on television.

Walter P. Chrysler

Brother Walter P. Chrysler (1875-1940), the automotive industry magnate for whom the famous car, company and building are named, began life modestly in Wamego, Kansas and went on to become one of the automotive industry's most notable figures. He often said he cared nothing for genealogy and even commented on the subject, "Ancestors, I have millions of them." However, with all his accomplishments, when asked for a biography for *Who's Who*, he specifically made note of the fact he was descended from Tuenis Van Dolsen, the first male child born on the island of Manhattan.

The Senior Junior Senator

Brother Ernest F. "Fritz" Hollings served over 38 years in the US Senate representing the State of South Carolina until his retirement in 2005. During that tenure, he served as the state's junior senator alongside Brother Strom Thurmond. The pair are the longest serving team of senators ever and Brother Thurmond's longevity gave Brother Hollings the somewhat dubious distinction of being the legislative body's most senior junior senator.

Fredericksburg Lodge

Fredericksburg Lodge 4 in Virginia provided no less than six Generals in the American Revolution: Hugh Mercer, Thomas Posey, Gustavus B. Wallace, George Washington, George Weedon and William Woodford.

Dedicated Preservationist

Thomas Armstrong, Jr., Lodge unknown, was a banker, attorney and president of the Arizona Archaeological and Historical Society. He was so dedicated to the preservation of historical sites that, in 1924, he purchased the Pueblo Grande Ancient Ruins and donated the grounds to the city of Phoenix.

Paul Revere And Old Ironsides

The *USS Constitution*, "Old Ironsides," is the world's oldest floating commissioned warship and is the home of Henry Knox Lodge, constituted under the Grand Lodge of Massachusetts. Its hull is constructed from 2,000 trees forming planks up to 7" thick. Brother Paul Revere, Past Grand Master of Massachusetts, forged hundreds of copper bolts holding the timbers in place as well as providing the ship's copper sheathing, spikes, pumps and anchors.

The Babe Ruth Of Table Tennis

Worshipful Brother James H. "Jimmy" McClure (1916 - 2005), member of Indianapolis' Oriental Lodge 500 (Now Evergreen-Oriental 500) is regarded as the greatest US table tennis player ever. In various divisions, "The Babe Ruth of Table Tennis" won six US and five world championships, and is the only American in the International Table Tennis Federation Hall of Fame.

Shibboleth

In the late 18th century, Barton Lodge in Ontario accepted "good merchantable wheat" as payment for dues.

Assassination Attempt

Awakened from an afternoon nap November 1, 1950, Brother Harry S. Truman, watched as two Puerto Rican nationalists stormed his residence in an attempt to assassinate him. A DC policeman, Leslie W. Coffelt, and one of the perpetrators, Griselio Torresola, died in the failed attempt. The other would-be assassin, Oscar Collazo was wounded in the melee and captured. A court convicted Collazo and sentenced him to death. President Truman, however commuted his sentence to life in prison and in 1979, President Jimmy Carter further reduced Collazo's sentence to time served, and he was freed. That year, Fidel Castro decorated Collazo as a hero. The guns used in the assassination attempt are on display at the Harry S. Truman Presidential Library in Independence, Missouri.

A Playful Student And A Stream Of Water

Harold E. "Doc" Edgerton of Aurora Lodge 68 in Nebraska, used stroboscopes to study synchronous motors for his doctoral thesis in electrical engineering at MIT in 1931. One day in his lab, he pointed his "strobe" at a stream coming out of a faucet and was amazed when he could see the individual drops of water. Brother Edgerton went on to become a professor at MIT and a giant in the electrical engineering field, but continued pointing his strobes at common objects and photographing them, developing the science of stroboscopic photography. He photographed bouncing balls, golf swings hummingbirds, bullets in flight and in general, anything that moved. Soon, Edgerton's photographs of everyday events were winning worldwide acclaim and, in 1937, the New York Museum of Modern Art featured his iconic photograph of a milk drop creating a coronet. Amazingly, today we remember this great scientist more for his artistic work, and it all started with a playful student and a stream of water.

Wheelock Commandery

Wheelock Commandery 5, Texas, ceased to exist when its 55 members joined the Confederate Army in 1861 and all were subsequently killed.

The First Airmail Letter

January 10, 1793, Jean Pierre Blanchard made the first US balloon flight. The event was such a big deal, Brother George Washington, US President, was in attendance. Blanchard did not speak English, so Washington provided him with a letter of introduction addressed to the owner of any property where Blanchard landed. Blanchard presented his letter when he landed in Deptford, Gloucester County, New Jersey, making Brother Washington the first person in the US to send an airmail letter.

The letter read: *"George Washington, President of the United States of America, to all to whom these presents shall come. The bearer hereof, Mr. Blanchard a citizen of France, proposing to ascend in a balloon from the city of Philadelphia, at 10 o'clock, A.M. this day, to pass in such direction and to descend in such place as circumstances may render most convenient — These are therefore to recommend to all citizens of the United States, and others, that in his passage, descent, return or journeying elsewhere, they oppose no hindrance or molestation to the said Mr. Blanchard; And, that on the contrary, they receive and aid him with that humanity and good will which may render honor to their country, and justice to an individual so distinguished by his efforts to establish and advance an art, in order to make it useful to mankind in general."*

"Given under my hand and seal at the city of Philadelphia, this ninth day of January, one thousand seven hundred and ninety three, and of the independence of America the seventeenth."

Light Horse Harry

Henry "Light Horse Harry" Lee, a member of Hiram Lodge 59 in Virginia, earned his nickname for his skill as a calvary captain during the revolutionary war. Having served as Virginia's Governor 1792-95, he gave the famous eulogy of Brother George Washington calling him, "First in war, first in peace and first in the hearts of his countrymen." Brother Lee was also the father of another famous soldier, Civil War General Robert E. Lee.

The First Shall Be Last...

Anson Jones (1798-1858), Holland Lodge 36, Houston (UD), was both the first Grand Master of the Grand Lodge of Texas (1838) and the Last President of the Republic of Texas (1844-1846). At the Battle of San Jacinto, Brother Jones carried the charter for Holland Lodge 36 in his saddlebags. Brother John M. Allen had delivered it to him only hours before on the prairie near San Jacinto.

The First Filibuster

Senator William R. King, a member of Phoenix Lodge 8 of Fayetteville, NC and later the 13th Vice President of the US, conducted the first sustained senate filibuster beginning February 18, 1841. It lasted 3 weeks, ending on March 11 and was in opposition to Senator Henry Clay's support of a bill to re-charter the Second National Bank. When Brother Clay (Grand Master of Kentucky in 1820) unsuccessfully attempted to change senate rules to block the

filibuster, a defiant Brother King suggested Clay "make his arrangements at his boarding house for the winter."

King won on both counts. The senate did not change its filibuster rules and those same rules substantially remain in effect today. The effort to re-charter the Second National Bank failed, as did the bank itself.

Raised And Demitted The Same Day

John Henry Brown (1820-1895), early Texas newspaper editor who served as mayor of both Dallas and Galveston, Texas, Was raised in Clarksville Lodge 17, Clarksville, Missouri, on March 1, 1845 and demitted on the same date.

Brother Brown wished to be raised in his home state of Missouri, but demitted so that he could return to Texas where he became one of the original signers for a charter of Victoria Lodge 40, Victoria, Texas.

Brother Washington's Death

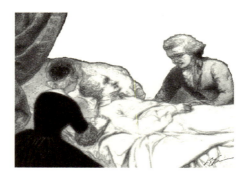

Brother George Washington's physician diagnosed his illness on his deathbed as "inflammatory quinsy." Modern medicine still debates what his illness actually might have been. Suffice it to say it was a form of throat infection. Brother Washington, would almost certainly have survived the affliction with today's medical techniques, perhaps with some simple treatment with antibiotics. Making a significant contribution to his death, however, was the fact that his doctors repeatedly used the accepted (at the time) technique of "bleeding" the President. During the ordeal, Washington's doctors took 124-126 ounces or 3.75 liters of his blood, which would have been more than half the blood in his body. This procedure almost certainly caused him to suffer profound shock. Ultimately he may have died anyway, but it is not an exaggeration to say that our beloved Brother and first President bled to death.

Sandusky, Ohio

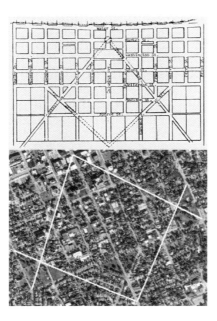

In 1818, Brother Hector Kilbourne, first Master of Science Lodge 50 (Ohio) was the surveyor who made the original plan for Sandusky, Ohio. Brother Kilbourne designed the city in the shape of a square and compasses laid out on an open Bible. Shown are his original plan and a current day satellite view of Sandusky. Science Lodge 50 is still an active Lodge today.

Teddy Bear

Brother Clifford K. Berryman (1869-1949) was Past Master of Temple Noyes Lodge 32 of Washington, DC, a Shriner and Knight Templar. A self-taught illustrator, he is thought to be the only political cartoonist ever to sketch every single member of any given congress. He is best known, however, for a single 1902 Washington Post cartoon captioned "Drawing the line in Mississippi." It alludes to a border dispute between Mississippi and Louisiana. In it, Brother Berryman depicts President Theodore "Teddy" Roosevelt showing compassion for a young bear cub. The concept of the "Teddy Bear" and the industry it spawned sprang from this single cartoon.

A New Sport

James Naismith, a member of Roswell Lee Lodge in Massachusetts and Lawrence Lodge 6 in Kansas, held degrees in philosophy, religion and physical education. He was also an ordained Presbyterian minister and Medical Doctor. Coaching track at the Springfield, Massachusetts YMCA in 1891, he was confronted with a class of rowdy boys with too much time on their hands in the winter. In an effort to channel his track team's energy constructively, he invented a new sport the athletes could play inside in cold weather. The object was to throw a "soft ball" into a peach basket. The basket was suspended 10 feet above the floor to prevent "rough protecting of the goal" as Brother Naismith had observed in other sports. The sport became very popular and proponents suggested naming it "Naismith Ball." Brother Naismith was too modest to accept that and instead named it after those suspended goals, calling it by its common name today: basketball.

The Covenant

George Washington, was torn by the fact that slavery was wrong, yet he remained a slave owner. Because of his grave reservations about the institution, he freed all of his slaves upon the death of his wife Martha. Martha, however, freed the slaves prior to that time, feeling with the covenant in her husband's will, her life might be in danger. Abagail Adams wrote of Martha's concern, "In the state in which they were left by the General, to be free at her death, she did not feel as tho her Life was safe in their hands, many of whom would be told that it was [in] their interest to get rid of her – She therefore was advised to set them all free at the close of the year."

His "Real" Job

Brother Richard C. "Dick" Harlow (1889-1962) had a spectacular career as a college football player and coach. He was the first non-alumnus to be head football coach at Harvard. Voted college coach of the year in 1936, Harlow has been recognized as a pioneer of modern defensive tactics. The fact that he compiled an overall record of 149–69–17 as head coach at Penn State, Western Maryland, Colgate and Harvard is made even more impressive by the fact that football coach wasn't his "real" job. Brother Harlow was actually a professor of zoology and was considered the country's foremost expert in the field of oology — the study of birds' eggs.

The Best Seller

Charles P. "Chic" Sale (1885-1936), Urbana Lodge 157 (IL), was an actor and humorist in vaudeville and a character actor in movies. He never achieved a great amount of fame, however, until he became an author and published *The Specialist*. The book sold 200,000 copies in three months and went on to be a million-seller. Its subject: outhouses. Considered risqué for its time, the book was nearly banned, but Brother Sale chose his words just carefully enough to avoid having it censored.

The Scapegoat

William Hull (1753-1825), a member of multiple Lodges and the first Master of Meridian Lodge in Natick, Massachusetts, was an officer in the American Revolution and a Brigadier General in the War of 1812. Defending Detroit in that war, he was forced to surrender when reinforcements and supplies failed to reach him. Made a scapegoat for these actions, Hull was tried, found guilty of cowardice and sentenced to death. In a bizarre twist,  the court then sent Brother Hull home to Newton, Massachusetts to await his execution! Upon receiving reports of the strange case, President James Madison realized Brother Hull had been set up and gave him a full pardon. History, indeed, regards William Hull as a hero, not a traitor.

Started The Gold Rush But Died Penniless

The man who discovered gold at Sutter's Mill and started the 1849 California Gold Rush, died penniless. Brother James W. Marshall found a nugget of gold while overseeing construction at the mill. The discovery brought thousands to the area in search of quick riches. The newcomers seized Marshall's property and divided it, leaving him in poverty. A bronze statue marks the spot where he discovered the gold. His Lodge is unknown, but he was a member of Sonora Chapter 2, RAM, Sonora, California.

No Experience Necessary

Gustavus V, King of Sweden, Nordiska Forsta Lodge, became Grand Master of Sweden on March 22, 1880 — at the age of 20.

Travelin' Man

Brother Theodore Roosevelt traveled to Panama in November, 1906 to view first-hand the progress on the construction of the Panama Canal. With that, he became the first US President to leave the country while still in office.

First African American Senator

Hiram Rhodes Revels was the first African American to serve in the US Senate and, for that matter, in congress. A Prince Hall Freemason, he served as Grand Chaplain of the Prince Hall Grand Lodge of Ohio. He was elected to the Senate from Mississippi to fill the unexpired term of Albert G. Brown, who withdrew from the office when Mississippi joined the Confederacy.
Brother Rhodes served a little over a year and went on to become President of what is today Alcorn State University.

The Penniless Oil Baron

Edwin L. Drake, Oil Creek Lodge 303 (now Titusville Lodge 754), drilled the world's first successful oil well in August of 1859. Seneca oil hired Drake to manage the project but the company was only halfheartedly committed to the effort. Seneca was so underfunded it hired Drake mainly because, as a former railroad employee, he had free use of the rails. When the project did not produce immediate results, Seneca bailed out and left Drake on his own. Brother Drake developed successful drilling techniques which are in use yet today, but failed to patent them and died penniless, having pioneered an industry that has made others billions.

Gander Memorial

On December 12, 1985, an Arrow Air charter flight crashed a half mile from the Gander airport shortly after takeoff, killing all 256 people on board, including 248 members of the US Army's 101st Airborne Division on their way home to NC for Christmas. It's the worst airplane disaster in Canada's history. The town built a memorial on the crash spot, a "larger-than-life sculpture of an unarmed soldier standing atop a massive rock, holding the hands of two small children each bearing an olive branch." The cost of the memorial was borne by the local Masonic fraternity and its ladies' auxiliary.

Lights Out

Brother Wyllis Cooper (1899-1955) created and directed the classic radio program "Lights Out" in 1933. The show was so popular it generated over 600 fan clubs, an astounding number at the time. Brother Cooper was so detail oriented that on one show he was not satisfied with the sound of a man being executed on a gallows, so he made the sound man drop through

the trap door and "hang himself" during the live broadcast. The sound man survived as did "Light's Out," which ran on radio through 1947 and later made the transition to television.

Dr. Elmer R. Arn

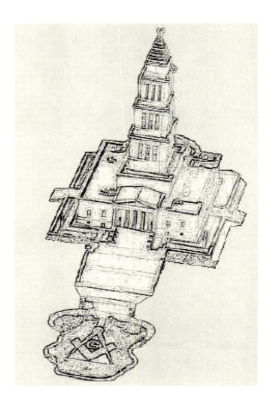

At his passing, the ashes of Dr. Elmer R. Arn (1886-1951), president of the George Washington Masonic National Memorial, were dropped by airplane on the memorial grounds. MWB Arn, a tireless supporter of the memorial, was the Grand Master of the Grand Lodge of Ohio 1935-36.

VP On Foreign Soil

William Rufus DeVane King, 13th Vice President of the US under Franklin Pierce, served virtually his entire term as VP on foreign soil. A member of Phoenix Lodge 8, Fayetteville, Brother King contracted tuberculosis prior to the election of 1852. After the campaign was over, his doctors advised him to go to Cuba to recuperate. He took the oath of office there by special act of congress.  His health continued to fail. He returned to the US, dying the following day, April 18, 1853, having served just 45 days in office.

Grand Lodge In The Ladies' Room

 On November 10, 1928, the cornerstone ceremony at the Masonic Lodge in Culver City, California, was so crowded, the Grand Master had to open the Grand Lodge in the ladies' room. Members reported the tyler had his work cut out for him during the meeting.

Daniel Boone, Freemason?

There are no existing records to indicate if frontiersman Daniel Boone was a Freemason. However, there is this report from his son Nathan on the occasion of his father's funeral,"Father's body was conveyed to Flanders Callaway's home at Charette, and there the funeral took place. There were no military or Masonic honors, the latter of which he was a member, as there were then but very few in that region of the country." So if his  son is to be believed, Daniel Boone was indeed a member of the fraternity.

Best Selling Single Of All Time

Working late one night in 1940, poolside at the Biltmore Hotel in Phoenix, Irving Berlin, Munn Lodge 190, New York City, told his secretary, "I just wrote the best song I've ever written — heck, I just wrote the best song anybody's ever written!" Brother Berlin was right on the mark. He had just finished composing *White Christmas*. Having sold 50 million copies — and counting — it is the best selling single of all time.

First Regular Female Freemason

Elizabeth Aldworth (1693-1772) of County Cork, Ireland and Catherine Sweet Babington (1815-1886) of Shelby, North Carolina, both became Freemasons under similar circumstances. Each overheard the conferring of degrees. The members of the Lodges involved, upon discovering the women, determined the best course of action was to initiate them, so as to protect the secrets by obligation. Ms. Aldworth had (possibly inadvertently) overheard a Fellowcraft Degree and was initiated in the second degree in 1712 at Lodge 44, Doneraile Court. Ms. Babington had repeatedly hidden in Lodge, had heard all degrees and was initiated as a Master Mason at the age of 16. Details surrounding Ms. Babbington's situation are sketchy, but generally thought to be true. Elizabeth Adlworth (Hon. Elizabeth St. Leger) most certainly became a Fellowcraft, and her grave marker recognizes her as the world's first regular female Freemason.

The Candidate

It is a well-known fact that John Hancock, Marchants Lodge 277 (Quebec) and St. Andrew's Lodge of Boston, was the first signer of the Declaration of Independence and wrote his name on that document in large bold letters, "So that George III may read it without putting on his glasses."  Less well-known are Hancock's other accomplishments including the fact that in 1789, he was a candidate for President of the US. In that era, political aspirations were considered demeaning, so Hancock did not campaign. He also knew General Washington would win easily and, if anything, Brother Hancock may have aspired to the Vice-Presidency. In the end, Hancock received only four electoral votes (in a system where each elector cast two votes). If by some quirk he had become president, other things being equal, he would have died in office on October 8, 1793.

Fellowship at 20° Below Zero

 Air pioneer and explorer, Brent Balchen, Norseman Lodge 878 of Brooklyn, dropped Masonic flags while flying over both the North and South Poles. In addition, He also dropped his Kismet Shrine fez on the South Pole while flying over it with Brother Richard Byrd in 1934. Later, he helped organize the Top Of The World Masonic Square Club in Thule, Greenland declaring, "Men need the fellowship and warmth of Masonry at 20° below zero."

The Boy Minister

William Mark Sexson, Bloomfield Lodge 84, Bloomfield, Indiana and Grand Master of Oklahoma in 1928, was Founder of the International Order of Rainbow for Girls. A Christian minister, he began his ministry at the age of 14 and incredibly, was fully ordained when he was only 17 years old.

Although Most Worshipful Brother Sexson was a Christian minister, he made it clear the IORG was an organization for girls of all faiths.

Four Presidents

Argentine Presidents and Masonic Brothers Justo José de Urquiza (1854-1860), Santiago Derqui (1860-1861), Bartolomé Mitre (1861-1868), Domingo Faustino Sarmiento (1868-1874). All were members of Union Del Plata Lodge 1 in Buenos Aries.

Four presidents were members of the same Lodge, but not in the US. Argentine Presidents Justo José de Urquiza (1854-1860), Santiago Derqui (1860-1861), Bartolomé Mitre (1861-1868) and Domingo Faustino Sarmiento (1868-1874) were all members of Union Del Plata Lodge 1 in Buenos Aries. But for a brief interim presidency in 1861, the four men would have served in succession.

Distinctions

Harland David Sanders (1890-1980), Hugh Harris Lodge 938, Corbin, Kentucky, was founder of the Kentucky Fried Chicken franchises. He became so much a part of the fabric of his home state of Kentucky that when he died his body lay in state in the rotunda of the Kentucky State Capitol and he was honored with a bust in the same building. Both are distinctions rarely bestowed on private citizens.

The First Lodge

Freemasonry began in the United States on July 30, 1733. On that date, Brother Henry Price and 18 other men met at the Bunch of Grapes Tavern on King Street in Boston and organized the Grand Lodge of Massachusetts, under the authority of Lord Montague, Grand Master of England. At the same meeting they instituted "The First Lodge," which today is St. John's Lodge.

From Shortest To Tallest

John Aasen, Highland Park Lodge 382, Los Angeles, was a 536 pound actor, occasionally billed as the world's tallest man. Estimates of his height range from about 7'3" to 8'11" but his actual height remains in doubt. Fifteen hundred Brothers attended his raising, which required the assistance of twelve craftsmen. A picture with Aasen and Brother Harold Lloyd standing together confirms Brother Aasen may have been in the range of eight feet tall, since Brother Lloyd was nearly six feet tall. Despite his extraordinary height, Brother Aasen was the shortest child in his Lutheran confirmation class.

Missouri's Emancipation Proclamation

Every schoolchild learns on January 1, 1863, President Abraham Lincoln issued the Emancipation Proclamation, declaring every slave in Confederate territory to be forever free. Lesser known is the fact that the state of Missouri also had a similar order. Thomas C. Fletcher, a member of Joachim Lodge 164 in Hillsboro, Missouri, was the state's first native-born governor. As his first major act after his election, Brother Fletcher issued Missouri's own Emancipation Proclamation on January 11, 1865.

Will The Real Thomas Hart Benton Please Stand Up

Will the real Thomas Hart Benton please stand up? Thomas Hart Benton (1782-1858), Missouri's first senator, was a Freemason who took such a strong stand against slavery in Missouri he was voted out of office. For this, he was featured in John F. Kennedy's *Profiles in Courage*. Thomas Hart Benton (1816-1879) was Grand Master of Iowa and a Union Civil War general credited with saving Albert Pike's Masonic library. Thomas Hart Benton (1889-1975), an artist, was not a Freemason, but painted the mural at the entrance to the Truman Presidential Library.

Senator Thomas Hart Benton

The three men were related. THB, the senator was the uncle of THB, the Grand Master and the great uncle of THB the painter.

The Lone Congressman

In 1903, Montana, as did all states, had 2 Untied States Senators. The area, however was so sparsely populated it only had one congressman. That unique honor went to Brother Joseph M. Dixon, Missoula Lodge 13. Dixon served as Montana's lone at-large congressman until 1907, when he became one of the state's US Senators. Brother Dixon also went on to become Master of his Lodge, Governor of Montana and was national chairman of the Bull Moose party when Theodore Roosevelt ran for US President on that ticket.

Buried Wrapped In An American Flag

Andrew Johnson (1808-1875), 17th President of the United States, Greeneville Lodge 119, Greeneville, Tennessee, was buried with his body wrapped in an American Flag and a copy of the US constitution beneath his head.

Brother Tom Mix

. Made 336 films, but only 9 were "talkies"
. Had five wives
. Was a bitter rival of Brother John Wayne
. Performed his own stunts in films
. Served as a pallbearer at Wyatt Earp's funeral — and wept
. Left films to join the circus, his real passion
. Put custom tires on all his cars with special tread that left his initials, TM, on the road
. Appears on the cover of The Beatles' *Sgt Pepper's Lonely Hearts Club Band* album
. Earned millions, spent millions
. Paid his first 10 years' dues the night he was raised at Utopia Lodge 537 of Los Angeles
. Was killed by a flying suitcase
. Had a star-studded funeral where Rudy Vallee sang "Empty Saddles"

Listerine

An English Baron and a renowned surgeon, Brother Joseph Lister (1827-1912) pioneered antiseptic surgery in the late 19th and early 20th centuries. Recognizing his medical accomplishments, Joseph Lister Lodge 8032 at University College Hospital in London is named in his honor. The general public, however, knows him more for the mouthwash named after him... Listerine.

City Of The Land Of The Indians

Jeremiah Sullivan (1794-1870), Union Lodge 2, Madison, Indiana, was a founder of Hanover College and the Indiana Historical Society. An attorney, he eventually became a justice of the Indiana Supreme Court. While a member of the state legislature in 1820, the Indiana Capital moved from Corydon to a new area, centrally located on the White River. Brother Sullivan proposed the name for the new city by combining the name of the state, Indiana ("land of the indians") and the Greek word for "city." giving the state capital its current name: Indianapolis.

Secretary For His Own Raising

Raised in Perseverance Lodge 782, Punjab, India in 1896, Brother Rudyard Kipling wrote the account of his own Raising for his Lodge. Raised by special dispensation at the age of 20 years, 6 months, his Lodge elected him secretary immediately after the ceremony.

Diogenes the Mason — 79 A.D.

In 1874, archaeologists discovered a room in Pompeii preserved from 79 A.D. in the ash of Mt. Vesuvius. Inside was a trestleboard, showing a large square above a skull and a plumb line. In the same room were an urn representing a pot of manna, a setting maul, trowel, spade, a small staff and a chest representing the Ark of the Covenant. Over the door of the house was an inscription, "Diogenes the Mason."

Oleo Rivers

Congressman L. Mendel Rivers, Landmark Lodge 76, Charleston, South Carolina, abhorred the tax on oleomargarine which congress passed under pressure from the dairy lobby to make margarine uncompetitive with butter. He campaigned so hard to have the tax repealed that he earned his trademark nickname, "Oleo" Rivers.

The Bet

Ruel C. Gridley (1829-1871), Civil War humanitarian and a member of 8 Masonic Lodges in 2 states, was born in Hannibal, Missouri, and was a boyhood friend of Mark Twain. During the Civil War, Brother Gridley bet a friend a sack of flour on the outcome of a political race. The loser was to carry the sack 1½ miles from Clifton to Austin, Nevada. Gridley lost and carried the load, followed by a brass band playing "John Brown's Body." At the end of the march Brother Gridley auctioned off the sack with proceeds going to the Sanitary Commission, a charitable organization benefiting sick and wounded soldiers. The buyer made the donation but didn't want the flour. So Brother Gridley shouldered his "sanitary sack of flour" and carried it throughout Nevada and California auctioning it over and over again. Ultimately he raised over $275,000 ($3.9 million in today's dollars) for his organization, which eventually became the primary forerunner to a much more well-known charity — the Red Cross.

Unsinkable

Virgil I. "Gus" Grissom. a member of Mitchell Lodge 228 in Mitchell, Indiana, was the second American to travel in space, making a suborbital flight on July 21, 1961. At the end of that flight, the escape hatch on his *Liberty Bell 7* space capsule blew and the vehicle sank. There was some  speculation, later proven false, that Brother Grissom had panicked and opened the door himself. Maintaining his sense of humor over the matter and much to the chagrin of NASA, Grissom named his next spacecraft *Molly Brown*, after the Broadway show *The Unsinkable Molly Brown*. When NASA balked at the name, Brother Grissom said he would name the craft *Titanic*. With that, NASA decided the name *Molly Brown* was just fine.

The Dinner

Upon the publication of his iconic book, *Up From Slavery*, Booker T. Washington, a Massachusetts Prince Hall Freemason, became the first African American to dine at the White House. Shortly after becoming president, Brother Theodore Roosevelt invited him to dinner amidst segregationist protests and some of the most vile and acerbic racial rhetoric in the history of the US.

The Star Spangled Banner

John Stafford Smith (1750-1836), Royal Somerset House & Inverness Lodge 4 of London, was the English composer who wrote the music for the US national anthem, *The Star Spangled Banner*. The popular belief is that Brother Smith originally wrote the song for the Anacreontic Society, a men's social club in London. There, it is said, *The Anacreontic Song* (or *To Anacreon in Heaven*), became a popular drinking song. Evidence suggests, however, Smith wrote the music prior to its use by the society, and it was originally used by an Irish Masonic orphans' home as its song.

In Defence of Fort McHenry

Dr. James McHenry (1753-1816), Spiritual Lodge 23 of Baltimore, was a friend and confidant of George Washington. He served as private secretary to both Washington and Lafayette, was an army surgeon, a member of the Constitutional Convention, a revolutionary war hero who became a prisoner of war, and served as the third US Secretary of War (1796-1800). In 1798, the US built a military fort in Baltimore and named it after him. It was a garrison that withstood an intense British attack during the War of 1812. During that attack, a US diplomat was aboard a British ship to negotiate a prisoner exchange. After watching the barrage and seeing an oversized American Flag raised the following morning to replace the tattered flag there, that diplomat wrote a poem describing the battle.

That poem by Francis Scott Key eventually became our national anthem, *The Star Spangled Banner*. Its original title was *In Defence of Fort McHenry*.

Antique Find

Found in an antique store in Creve Coeur, Missouri. *For Every Boy Who's on the Level There's A Girl Who's on the Square*, published in 1920, words and music by Harry Pease, Ed. G. Nelson and Gilbert Dodge. Cover art by E. H. Pfeiffer.

Hoot

Edward R. "Hoot" Gibson, Truth Lodge 628 of Los Angeles, had roles in dozens of films and is considered one of the pioneer cowboy movie actors. Famous for his acting, Brother Gibson was first and foremost a star performer on the rodeo circuit who, among many other honors, won the steer roping World Championship at the Calgary Stampede in 1912.

The Right Place At The Right Time

He took the most famous and historic film of the 20th century. Because he was a Freemason, anti-Masonic groups and other fringe organizations have maintained Abraham Zapruder (1905 - 1970) was standing in Dealey Plaza on November 22, 1963 to "document" the assassination of President John F. Kennedy, allegedly knowing in advance what would happen. In reality, he happened to be standing in the right place at the right time to create a lasting record of a tragic but historically important event.

Mayo Clinic

The original Mayo Clinic started in a Masonic Temple in Rochester, Minnesota, where William Worrall Mayo (1819-1911), Charles H. Mayo (1865-1939) and Charles W. Mayo (1898-1968) were members.

One Tough Guy

Theodore Roosevelt, a member of Matinecock Lodge 806 in Oyster Bay, New York, was shot while preparing to deliver a campaign speech on October 14, 1912. The bullet passed through his glasses case and his folded 50-page speech prior to hitting him. The items in his pocket probably slowed it enough to save his life. Amazingly, Brother Roosevelt went on to deliver the 90-minute speech prior to going to the hospital. The bullet remained inside him for the rest of his life.

Only Doing My Duty

President William McKinley decided to become a Freemason when he saw acts of compassion by a Union soldier toward Confederate prisoners during the Civil War. The Union Brother who extended the kindness told McKinley, "It makes no difference to me; they are Brother Masons in trouble and I am only doing my duty."

A Fervent Socialist

The Reverend Francis J. Bellamy (1855-1931) was the author of the Pledge of Allegiance to the American Flag. A Baptist minister, he was a member of Little Falls Lodge 181 in New York. In 1955, The Order of the Eastern Star erected a tablet to honor his memory at its home in Oriskany, NY. It is usually a surprise to most to learn Bellamy, who authored the pledge for a country that is a hallmark of free enterprise and capitalism, was also a fervent socialist.

Godspeed, John Glenn

On February 20, 1962, John Glenn became the first American to orbit the earth in his space capsule, *Friendship 7*, blasting off with his flight crew wishing him, "Godspeed, John Glenn." At flight's end an indicator light warned his heat shield was loose. Glenn therefore kept his retrorockets in place to secure the heat shield and returned to earth in what he described as "a real fireball." Interestingly, the rocket which carried him aloft was a converted nuclear missile. Brother Glenn is a member of Concord Lodge 688 Concord, Ohio.

A Strong Calling

Lost and searching for a purpose in life, young Peter Marshall, Old Monkland St. James Lodge 177, Coatbridge, Scotland, walked into a fog-shrouded woods to pray for guidance. As he moved deeper into the forest, the trees blocked the light and the fog thickened, rendering him nearly blind. All the while praying for God to give him direction in his life, he continued to walk visionless. Suddenly, he stumbled on a tree root and fell. Unhurt, he found himself lying on the ground staring into an abyss. He was at the edge of a sheer cliff and realized had he kept walking he would have dropped to a certain death. At that moment he knew God had saved him with what he later called "a strong calling." Then and there he dedicated himself to the Lord's service. Brother Peter Marshall went on to move to the the US, create a great ministry and eventually become chaplain of the US Senate. Called home to the Lord at the young age of 46, Brother Marshall's wife Catherine immortalized his ministry in her best seller, *A Man Called Peter*.

Dew It With Dewey

The first political campaign T-Shirt originated with the 1948 election to promote the presidential bid of Brother Thomas Dewey, urging voters to... "Dew it with Dewey."

A Profile In Courage

Missouri's first Senator, Brother Thomas Hart Benton (1782 - 1858), maintained a strong Unionist stance in a predominantly pro-slavery, pro-South state. Because of this unpopular view, he ultimately lost the senate seat he had held for thirty years. For this unyielding and courageous stance, John F. Kennedy selected Benton as one of only eight men worthy of inclusion in his heralded book, *Profiles in Courage*.

Scopes Monkey Trial

William Jennings Bryan, US Secretary of State, presidential candidate, Lincoln Lodge 19, Nebraska, may be best known for prosecuting and winning the 1925 "Scopes Monkey Trial." In what was one of the great media circuses of the 20th century, the court found John T. Scopes guilty of teaching evolution in a high school science class. Six years earlier, in 1919, Brother Bryan gave the commencement address at the high school in Salem, Illinois. In the audience on that occasion was graduating high school senior John T. Scopes.

Outstanding Sportsman

John W. Galbreath, University Lodge 631 of Columbus, Ohio, made a fortune in commercial property development. His business successes, however, were only a means that allowed him to pursue his real passion: sports. He owned both the Pittsburgh Pirates baseball team and Darby Dan racing stables. As an owner he won three World Series (1960, 1971, 1979) and two Kentucky Derbies (1963, 1967). Named Outstanding Breeder in 1974, He is one of only four owners to win both the Kentucky Derby and Epson Derby. Oddly, or perhaps as a premonition, this winner of so many derbies was born in Derby, Ohio.

The Argonaut

Simon Lake, a member of New Jersey's Monmouth Lodge 172, built the first working submarine, the Argonaut, in 1897. He founded the Lake Submarine Company, making a career out of building submarines and consulting to governments wanting to manufacture them. Even before the  turn of the century he had a design so sophisticated he developed a unit with locking chambers so divers could enter and exit the craft.

The Clerical Error

Brother Robert G. Harrison, Noblesville Lodge 57, Indiana, became inadvertently embroiled in a presidential assassination attempt due to a clerical error!

As a senior executive at Wallace Expanding Machines in Indianapolis, Brother Harrison's biography appeared in the Standard and Poor's Directory of Corporate Executives. A clerical  error in his listing said he was also the Chairman and CEO of US Natural Resources, Inc., a company that, in spite of its environmentally-friendly sounding name, was involved in clearing forests. On September 5, 1975, fanatic environmentalist and Manson disciple Lynette "Squeaky" Fromme went to a Gerald Ford rally to plead with him on behalf of her environmental causes. In the process she pointed a gun at Brother Ford, earning a life prison sentence for the attempted assassination of the President. In the ensuing investigation, authorities searched Fromme's apartment and found a mailing containing one of her rants. She used Brother Harrison's home as the return address due to what she thought was his involvement with USNR. A quick but exciting conversation with the FBI subsequently cleared Brother Harrison of any involvement.

Lodge Operative

Chartered May 7, 1781, Lodge Operative 150 of Aberdeen, Scotland consisted only of Brothers who were or had been operative Masons. For years, many of its members traveled to build stone structures worldwide, especially in the USA. Although today the Lodge no longer consists exclusively of operative Masons, it honors its heritage. Each year it installs its incoming Master with an apron given to a traveling Brother coming back from the US in the early 20th century. The apron bears the insignia of a US Master and is used to honor Lodge Operative's role in the "American trade." The Brothers of the Lodge have left its legacy throughout the world. According to its documentation, Lodge Brothers have played a significant role in erecting the following stone edifices: The Paris Opera House, the London Bridge, the Sydney Harbor Bridge, the State Capital Building in Texas, the foundations and lower level of

Freemasons Hall in Edinburgh, the Marischal College (the second largest granite building in the world) and many others.

First Masonic Book In America

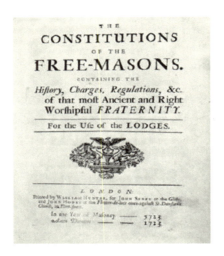

The first Masonic Book in America was Benjamin Franklin's edition of Anderson's Constitutions. MWB Franklin published the book in 1734, the same year he became Grand Master of Pennsylvania.

Beloved

A poll in the mid 1960s recognized the two most beloved Americans as Abraham Lincoln and Will Rogers. Brother Rogers was a member of Claremore Lodge 53, McAlester Consistory and the Tulsa Shrine, all located in Oklahoma.

Fala

Franklin Delano Roosevelt is the only US President depicted with his pet in an official government memorial. Brother Roosevelt's dog, Fala, appears in the Franklin Delano Roosevelt Memorial, Washington, DC.

A Disarming Quip

After reigning over seven years as world heavyweight boxing champion, Jack Dempsey stepped into the ring against contender Gene Tunney in September of 1926. Brother Dempsey, Kenwood Lodge 800, Chicago, was the heavy favorite in the fight, but the younger, quicker Tunney won in a decision, after a brutal contest. Back in his dressing room, Dempsey's wife, actress Estelle Taylor, was worried about her battered husband's condition, but the bruised boxer eased her concerns with a quick quip that made the papers the next day.

Years later, President Ronald Reagan, an honorary member of the Scottish Rite and Shrine, became the only president in office to be wounded and survive an assassination attempt. Having been rushed to the hospital, Reagan's wife, former actress Nancy Davis, was similarly worried about her husband's condition. Reagan eased her concerns by quoting Brother Dempsey, with the same disarming quip he had used over a half century earlier:

"Honey, I forgot to duck."

The Most Daring Act Of The Age

On February 16, 1804, Brother Stephen Decatur, Jr. (1779-1820) led a naval expedition into enemy waters that British Admiral Horatio Nelson called "the most daring act of the age." In an effort to curtail piracy in Tripoli Harbor, President Thomas Jefferson had dispatched an expeditionary force to the area. The US Frigate *Philadelphia* had gone aground, and the enemy captured the vessel. Fearing the pirates would use the frigate against the US as well as using it as a model to build better ships, the president sent Brother Decatur on a mission to destroy it. Decatur disguised himself and his men as Maltese sailors, entered Tripoli Harbor undetected in a small two-mast ship, boarded the *Philadelphia*, defeated the pirates on board, destroyed the frigate and left without losing a single American. Decatur was initiated October 12, 1799 in St. Johns Lodge, Baltimore.

A Tough Job, But Somebody's Got To Do It

California's Catalina Lodge 524 (now Temecula-Catalina Freemason Lodge 524) at one time had an official "Clock Winder."

Long John

Put into service during the Civil War era, *Long John* was Chicago's first fire engine. A spiffy new steam-powered model, the amazing vehicle was named for Chicago's mayor "Long John" Wentworth. Brother Wentworth, a member of Chicago's Oriental Lodge 33, introduced the fire engine during his term as mayor and, in turn, the city named it in his honor. Considered a near-giant in a time when the average man stood 5'7", 300 pound "Long John," at 6'6" towered over most people of his day.

A Forgotten Brother

His father was Sam Houston's Lt. Governor. His uncle died at the Alamo. At 28, Brother Ahijah W. "A.W.' Grimes (1850-1878) was a promising deputy sheriff when notorious outlaw Sam Bass murdered him in cold blood in a general store, where Grimes was investigating Bass' suspicious activity. Another lawman fatally wounded Bass as he tried to escape. Buried in the same cemetery, Bass' fame and legend grew after his death. Several yards away from Bass' grave, Brother Grimes' memorial reads, "Gone but not forgotten."

Unfortunately the broken, weathered tombstone and history's fading memory of Brother Grimes' heroism tell a different story.

Although a road and medical building have been named there for Grimes, the real town hero in Round Rock, Texas, remains Sam Bass. Each year the town stages a "Sam Bass Shootout." Sadly, the cemetery where both are buried is located on Sam Bass Road.

Oscar Of The Waldorf

Oscar Tschirky (1866-1950), a member of Metropolitan Lodge 273 of New York City, was at one time the most famous chef in the world. Known as "Oscar of the Waldorf," he was the author of a best-selling cookbook and was the creator of the Waldorf Salad. Various accounts give him credit for popularizing Thousand Island dressing and originating Eggs Benedict. Historians agree, the Waldorf-Astoria did not  make Brother Oscar famous. Rather, he made the hotel famous. He was so well-known many claim when Hollywood came up with a statuette to honor its best actors, some thought it looked like him, albeit younger and thinner, and they called it "Oscar." All this, despite the fact that Brother Oscar Tschirky was the Waldorf's *maître d'hôtel*. He was not a chef!

Swimming Pool Press Conference

One of the most athletic of US Presidents, Brother Gerald Ford swam daily and once gave a presidential press conference while swimming in the White House swimming pool.

Trigger

Some think it's an urban legend, but it isn't. Roy Rogers, famed TV and movie cowboy, and a member of Hollywood Lodge 355, really did have his beloved palomino horse Trigger stuffed (actually stretched over a plaster cast) and mounted when Trigger died in 1955. Brother Rogers also commissioned a 24-foot statue of Trigger to sit outside his museum. The mold for that statue also served as the mold for "Bucky the Bronco," which sits outside the Denver Bronco's football stadium. In 2009, the "stuffed" Trigger sold for $266,000 to television channel RFD-TV, which plans to start a Western museum in Omaha. Roy's famous dog Bullet was also stuffed and will stand there alongside Trigger. When the Roy Rogers museum in Branson closed in 2010, developers bought the statue outside for display at the new Apple Valley Village, near Rogers' home.

Brother Perkins' Amazing Contraption

The nearly-forgotten Jacob Perkins (1766-1849), St. Peter's Lodge, Newburyport, Massachusetts, was such a prolific inventor he probably ranks with the likes of Benjamin Franklin or Thomas Edison. Among his inventions were coinage dies, the first refrigerator, a machine for making nails, improved engraving plates, a "bathometer" to measure the depth of water and a "pleometer" to mark with precision the speed with which a vessel moved through water. He also engraved England's first adhesive-backed postage stamp, the famous "penny black." Perhaps his most intriguing invention, however, was the ridiculous-sounding steam gun. Demonstrations of the amazing contraption fascinated the public. The weapon was capable of shooting 1,000 rounds per minute and could penetrate its ball-shaped projectiles through eleven one-inch pine boards at a distance of 35 yards. Perkins even invented an accessory that allowed the gun to shoot around corners, a derivative of which was used in World War II. In other words, in a day when muskets fired a single bullet and required a tedious reloading process, Brother Perkins invented the ultimate weapon. The military, however, although impressed by the gun's overwhelming firing power and accuracy, rejected it because it was so powerful it deformed the bullets,

His Mark

Companion William F. "Buffalo Bill" Cody, a Mark Master in North Platte, Nebraska, not surprisingly selected a buffalo head as his personal mark.

A Premature Honor

William Hesketh Lever Lodge 2916 at Port Sunlight, England, was named to honor a soap manufacturer (founder of Lever Brothers/Unilever) BEFORE he was initiated. The Lodge was consecrated June 4, 1902. Lever was its first initiate the following July 8th.

Stuck

William Howard Taft, a member of Kilwinning Lodge 365 in Cincinnati, Ohio, was a huge man at 6'2" and 340 pounds. Very athletic, he never let his weight affect him much until he was bathing in the White House one evening and became hopelessly stuck in the tub. It took several staffers and lots of butter to extract him. After that adventure, Brother Taft had a much larger tub installed, one which he could use without incident, and which could hold four ordinary sized men.

Not Bad For An Evening's Work

Frank Land, founder of DeMolay and an accomplished artist, designed the DeMolay crest. This is not a surprise until noted that he designed the crest in 1908, fully eleven years before DeMolay existed. He sketched it's original design one evening in art class upon becoming disinterested in the instructor's still-life assignment. The instructor's sister, Nell Swiezwski, caught him goofing off. As sometimes happens, one thing led to another and Brother Land married Nell. In one evening Frank Land had designed an emblem for a future worldwide organization and met his future bride. Not bad for an evening's work.

Elbridge Gerry's Redistricting Scheme

Elbridge Gerry (1744-1814), Philanthropic Lodge of Marblehead, Massachusetts, was a signer of the Declaration of Independence, fifth Vice President of the US, Governor of Massachusetts, a congressman, a delegate to the Constitutional Convention of 1787 and more. He is mainly remembered, however, for his efforts to redistrict Massachusetts in an attempt to keep Republicans in power, a tactic which political parties have employed since. His actions sparked such controversy at the time that his contemporary pundits named the process after him: Gerrymandering.

His Favorite Prose

Brother Edwin T. Booth was the Brother of Lincoln's assassin, John Wilkes Booth. However, he should be remembered for much more, including the fact that he once saved the life of Robert Lincoln, the President's son. Brother Edwin was a member of New York Lodge 330. A renowned Shakespearean actor, Brother Edwin was once asked what he considered his favorite prose. In answering, he asked the audience to stand and then he repeated the Lord's Prayer.

The Square And Compasses Brand

The first livestock brand registered in the state of Montana was the Square and Compasses brand, issued February 10, 1873, to Poindexter and Orr. Today, Koch Industries still uses the brand, and has donated one of the original irons to the Grand Lodge of Montana.

3,580 Mile Swim

Paul Boyton (1848-1924), Lodge of Friendship 206, London, was a world-famous adventurer and swimmer. He opened the world's first permanent amusement park in Chicago in 1894 and the following year established what would become the Coney Island amusement park. As a stunt swimmer, he invented a rubberized floating "wet suit," using it to swim long distances. He first used it to cross the English Channel and in 1881 used it to swim the Missouri River from Cedar Creek, Montana to St. Louis, Missouri, a distance of 3,580 miles.

The (Masonic) Republic Of Texas

All four presidents of the Republic of Texas were Master Masons. David G. Burnet (President in 1836) was a member of

Holland Lodge 1 of Houston; Sam Houston (President 1836-38 and 1841-44) was a member of at least four Lodges including Cumberland Lodge 8 of Nashville, Tennessee; Mirabeau B. Lamar (President 1838-41) was a member of Harmony Lodge 6 of Galveston; and Anson Jones (President 1844-46) was the first Grand Master of the Grand Lodge of Texas.

I Shot Him, Sir

Prior to becoming political allies, Missouri's cantankerous and imposing first senator Thomas Hart Benton and Andrew Jackson were bitter foes. Believing Jackson had insulted his brother Jesse, Benton hunted Jackson down. A fight erupted ending in gun-play in which Benton shot and nearly killed Jackson. After the death of Andrew Jackson, a young colleague approached Senator Benton. The novice politician asked Benton if he had known Jackson. Benton replied in his familiar, pompous manner, "Yes, sir, I knew him, sir; General Jackson was a very great man, sir. I shot him, sir!"

Grounded

Brother John Glenn, Concord Lodge 688 Concord, Ohio, became the first American to orbit the earth on February 20, 1962. Immediately recognized as one of the greatest American heroes of the time, the ticker-tape parade in New York held in his honor equaled in size only that of Brother Charles Lindbergh. Afterward, the city reported it had picked up a record 3,474 tons of confetti. Brother Glenn never flew again during the early space program. Reports say officials grounded him because they felt in the event of a mishap, the loss of such a great American hero would irreparably damage the space program as well as the morale of the American public.

US President For One Day

Brother David Rice Atchison's grave marker proclaims his status as President of the United States.

Because inauguration day fell on a Sunday, President-elect Zachary Taylor and Vice-President-elect Millard Fillmore both refused to take their oaths of office, leaving the presidency vacant. Constitutionally, succession fell to the President of the Senate, Brother David Rice Atchison, a member of Missouri's Platte Lodge 56. Judge Willie Magnum administered the oath of office and for a single day, Sunday, March 4, 1849, Brother David Rice Atchison was, by some accounts, the President of the United States.

Handle With Care

In 1921, President Warren G. Harding, Marion Lodge 70, Marion, Ohio, honored Marie Curie for her achievements in the world of science. Madame Curie, the first person honored with two Nobel Prizes (in chemistry and physics), was a pioneer researcher on radioactivity. To commemorate her work in the field, Brother Harding presented her with a gram of highly radioactive radium!

Allies And Enemies

Emilio Aguinaldo, Philippine patriot and general, led the only forces ever directly to fight as both allies and enemies of the United States. He supported the US in the Spanish-American war, but became suspicious of the US after the war and led his forces in rebellion against US dominance. Defeated in that effort he eventually became a staunch supporter of the US. Initiated January 1, 1895, in Pilar Lodge under the Grand Orient of Spain, where he eventually became Master, Brother Aguinaldo retired after the uprising. He organized Magdalo Lodge, which met at his residence. Upon his death in 1964, he had been a Freemason for over 69 years.

Highest Masonic Lodge

The highest Masonic Lodge on earth is Roof of the World Lodge 1094 in Oroya, Peru. It's elevation has been measured to be approximately 14,167 feet. The next highest Lodge is thought to be Corinthian Lodge 35, at 10,152 feet in Leadville, Colorado.

The Lodge Of Generals

Although at the time it had only 50 members, Miner's Lodge 273 in Galena, Illinois, supplied no less than five Generals to the Union effort in the Civil war. Among them were Brothers Ely Parker (A Seneca Indian), John Rawlings, William Rowley and John Corson Smith. Brother Rawlings later became US Secretary of War and Brother Smith went on to become Illinois' Grand Master.

Thayendanegea

Joseph Brant (Thayendanegea), Mohawk Chief and later Chief of the Six Nations, was the first recorded Native American Freemason. Somewhat controversial because of his efforts as a warrior and soldier, Brant is known to have spared at least four Brothers who made an appeal to him with the Grand Hailing Sign of Distress. Raised in Hiram's Cliftonian Lodge 417, London, WB Brant was also the first Master of Lodge 11, Brantford,  Mohawk Village. In 1787, Brother Brant translated and published the Gospel of Mark into the Mohawk language. In 1807, he died and was buried near what today is the town of Burlington, Ontario. In 1850, several young tribesmen carried his remains in a 34 mile relay from his original grave site to the Chapel of the Mohawks in Brantford, where it rests today.

Number 33

Scottie Pippen, standout NBA player for the Chicago Bulls had a distinguished professional and college basketball career. He is also one of the most well-known contemporary Prince Hall Freemasons. As one might expect, conspiracy theorists have had a field day with the fact that Pippen wore the number 33 throughout his career, overlooking the fact that he wore that number long before he was a Freemason.

Flying Lessons

Merrill C. Meigs, a member of Welcome Lodge 916, Chicago and the aviation pioneer for whom Chicago's Meigs Field is named, once gave Brother Harry Truman a series of flying lessons.

The Lewis And Clark Trail

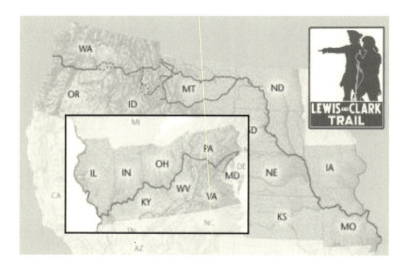

Brothers Meriwether Lewis and William Clark set out on May 21, 1804 from St. Charles, in what is now Missouri. Their "Voyage of Discovery" took them to the west coast, laying the groundwork to open the vast, rich west for the young United States. The journey actually started, however, in Washington DC months earlier, when Brother Lewis began his trip to the Mississippi River. Today's Lewis and Clark Trail, a series of parks and roads that roughly follows their route, reflects that fact by running from Washington, DC to the Oregon shore.

Shaq

NBA standout Shaquille O'Neal, a member of MWPH Widow's Son Lodge 28 in Boston is primarily known for his skills as a basketball star, movie actor and even a rap artist. He has also, however, maintained a dedicated interest in law enforcement. A graduate of the Los Angeles County Sheriff's Reserve Academy, he is a sworn reserve officer with the Los Angeles Port Police and the Miami Beach police force, where his annual salary is $1.00. In 2005, he played an active role in discovering, tracking down and capturing two suspects involved in a hate crime.

Costa Rica

Father Francisco Calvo, a Jesuit Priest, traveled to Peru in 1865. There a group of Catholic priests introduced him to Freemasonry. Father Calvo was so impressed by the Craft, he was initiated, returned home to Costa Rica and founded Freemasonry in that country. Brother Calvo went on to establish Lodge Caridad 26, where he became Master. He was instrumental in founding the Scottish Rite in Costa Rica and became its first Sovereign Grand Commander, serving in that position until his death nearly 25 years later.

The Hexagon On Saturn

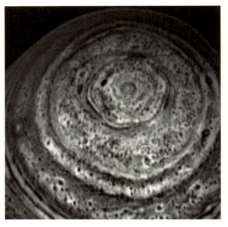

A naturally-occurring, permanent hexagon exists at the north pole of the planet Saturn. Determined to be a resonance-based phenomenon, this feature has nonetheless not escaped the scrutiny of certain Masonic detractors who are certain it is one of the great sources of Masonic mysticism and power. Except for those making such claims, the precise relationship between the Saturnian polygon and Masonic practices is too complex for anyone to understand, including the Freemasons themselves. The Masons, on the other hand, expose their conspiratorial nature by denying the Saturn hexagon has anything to do with their organization, if for no other reason than the fact that Masons who have been to Saturn report the weather there is too inclement for their frequent family picnics.

Wild Bill Hickok's Chair

This chair comes from Amazonia Lodge in northwest Missouri, near the Kansas Border. Amazonia 320 received its charter in 1890 and consolidated with Savannah 71 in 1907. Although the fact that James Butler "Wild Bill" Hickok was a Mason is in doubt, local lore says he often attended meetings at Amazonia. The chair is on display at the Masonic Museum in Columbia, Missouri.

The Alamo

The Alamo fell March 6, 1836. Freemasons Davy Crockett, Jim Bowie, William B. Travis and others died in the battle, defending the Republic of Texas against Mexican troops. Weeks later at the Battle of San Jacinto cries of "Remember the Alamo" spurred soldiers on as Texas won its independence.

Anticipating His Masonic Future

It's a puzzle that Ulysses S. Grant (1822-1885), eighteenth President of the United States, never became a Mason. His father, Jesse R. Grant, was a member of Bethel Lodge 61, Bethel, Ohio. His father-in-law, Lewis Dent, was a member of Amith Lodge 5, Zanesville, Ohio. Further, perhaps in anticipation of a Masonic future, his parents gave him a very Masonic name. His real name was Hiram Ulysses Grant.

The Gift He Never Received

Luke A. Lockwood (1833-1905), first Master of Acacia Lodge 85 at Greenwich, Connecticut, was a Masonic author and Grand Master of Connecticut in 1872. In 1905, his Lodge arranged a gala celebration of his 50-years of Masonry by purchasing a $1,000 silver service (worth $25,000 in today's dollars) to give him on that occasion. MWB Lockwood never received the gift, dying unexpectedly just prior to the ceremony.

The Exception

From its founding as a state in 1890, until the mid-twentieth century, every governor of Wyoming was, with one exception, a Freemason. The Exception? Nellie Tayloe Ross, the first woman governor in the United States. Ms. Ross' husband, however was a Freemason. In fact, he was William B. Ross, who preceded her as Governor. When her husband died in office, supporters urged her to become a candidate to replace him. Although Ms. Ross refused to campaign, she was elected by a wide margin. Born near St. Joseph, Missouri, Ms. Ross was a member of the Order of the Eastern Star.

Rejected!

The Marines and Paratroopers both rejected him, thinking he wouldn't be a good soldier because he was too small. When the Army finally accepted him in the infantry, Brother Audie Murphy, North Hollywood Lodge 542, California, proved them all wrong, becoming the most decorated hero of World War II.

Is Prince Hall On The $2 Bill?

An urban legend suggests a depiction of Brother Prince Hall appears on the back of the two dollar bill. The back of the bill shows an etching drawn from John Trumbull's painting, *Declaration of Independence*. In the etching, a dark-complected figure sits in the middle of the front row of seated delegates at the Second Continental Congress and some believe this must be Prince Hall. However, for all his accomplishments, Brother Prince Hall, as a historical fact, was not present at that meeting. It turns out the dark complexion of the man in question is a product of the etching. Further examination of the painting from which the etching has its origin shows the person sitting in that position to be Robert Morris.

Gentle Giant

Acclaimed as the world's strongest man, Michael Dorizas of Philadelphia Lodge 51 literally walked around the world, surviving a revolt in Turkey and overcoming bandits in both Russia and China. A three-time Olympian, the gentle giant earned a Ph.D and taught geography at the University of Pennsylvania. From 1914-1916, Brother Michael was undefeated intercollegiate heavyweight wrestling champion.

Amazingly, he pinned every single opponent he faced in less than a minute.

First Physician and First Master

Aaron Elliott was the first physician west of the Mississippi River. He was also the first Master of a Lodge west of the Mississippi, Louisiana Lodge 109. The Grand Lodge of Pennsylvania chartered the Lodge in 1808 in Ste. Genevieve, in what would become the state of Missouri.

Lodge Chests

In 19th century Ireland it was a common practice for Lodges to keep their valuables, including money, paraphernalia and jewels in Lodge chests. Each chest had three locks with the Master, Senior Warden and Junior Warden each holding a key. This practice required all three officers to be present at every meeting or any other time the chest was opened.

Adding Fuel To The Fire

The Grand Lodge of Pennsylvania dedicated its second home, located on Chestnut Street in Philadelphia, in 1809. A magnificent building for its time, the Philadelphia Masonic Hall was one of that city's landmarks until March 9, 1819. On that evening, as Washington Lodge 59 was meeting there, a chimney fire swept through the building, completely destroying it. No one was hurt, and Lodge members saved some property by carrying it out of the building, but much was lost as the fire erupted into what was described as "a great conflagration." Reports say the inferno became so intense it was visible in New Castle, Delaware, 32 miles away. A letter from Rebecca Gratz (1781-1869), who lived next door, describes the incident in detail. In it, she makes it clear the building might have been saved but for the fact that the volunteer firemen who came to fight the fire were drunk! As the evening progressed and it became clear the Masonic Hall was lost and Ms. Gratz' house was safe, the event became almost festive as Ms. Gratz added fuel to the fire — pun intended — by serving alcoholic beverages to the fire fighters.

The Racin' Mason

Sam Hornish Jr., Omega Lodge 564, Defiance, Ohio, won the 2006 Indianapolis 500 Mile Race. Some have labeled his victory the single most exciting moment in the history of the "Greatest Spectacle in Racing." Running second for several laps, Brother Hornish made a spectacular pass with less than 1/4 mile remaining to win the classic race by a matter of inches.

Lost in the hubbub of his breathtaking victory was the fact that Brother Hornish also won the race's sportsmanship award, reflecting his character as a Freemason. It was the first time the sportsmanship award had ever gone to the winner of the great race.

First Italian Freemason

Giuseppe Garibaldi, the Great Italian Liberator, was Grand Master of Italy who also held the title of "First Italian Freemason." During World War II, Italy's tyrannical dictator Benito Mussolini removed all Masonic references from the great monument to Brother Garibaldi in Rome, replacing them with Fascist symbols. After the war, authorities replaced the propaganda on the monument with the original Masonic pieces.

Father Of Missouri Schools

In 1812, Thomas Fiveash Riddick personally rode on horseback, at his own expense, from St. Louis to Washington, D.C. in support of a bill that gave all unclaimed lands to the public school system. The bill passed and ensured a sound future for Missouri public schools. Riddick went on to become the first Grand Master of the Grand Lodge of Missouri and today is known as the father of the Missouri public school system.

The West Bank Of The Hudson River

Alexander Hamilton (1755-1804), first Secretary of the Treasury, had two sons, both named Philip. Philip the younger (1802-1884) was assistant District Attorney in New York and was a member and Past Master of Albion Lodge 26. He was often confused with his older brother of the same name who died prior to the second Philip's birth. The elder Philip (1782-1801) died in a

duel with George I. Eacker. Philip challenged Eacker to the duel on the west bank of the Hudson River in Weehawken, New Jersey, for insulting his father. Three years later, Alexander Hamilton died from a fatal wound in a duel with Vice President Aaron Burr, held on the same spot where his son Philip had died.

Alexander Hamilton's Masonic affiliation is in doubt. He was recorded as having visited American Union Lodge in Morristown, New Jersey, on December 27, 1779, when Washington is supposed to have raised General Lafayette. Some speculate it may have been someone else with the same name. Hamilton also is said to appear standing next to George Washington in the painting *The Petition*, which depicts the presentation of a petition to Brother Washington to become Grand Master of the United States.

Great Things

In the French-Indian War, Brother George Washington was shot no less than five times in a single battle. His thick coat stopped four of the bullets and one went through his hat. If that wasn't enough, in the same battle he had two horses shot out from under him. Observing this, one Indian Chief said he thought Washington's God must be protecting him so that he could go on to do great things.

A Startling Discovery

Worshipful Brother Edward Jenner, Royal Faith and Friendship Lodge 270 of Berkeley, England, made a startling discovery in 1789. He observed milkmaids who contracted cowpox did not get the associated disease, smallpox. The announcement of his discovery led to vaccinations and changed medicine forever.

Misnamed?

How can Wellesley College be named after Brother Henry Fowle Durant (1822-1881)? Durant founded Wellesley College (Massachusetts) in 1870, naming it after himself. His original name was Henry Welles Smith, but Brother Durant legally changed it, thinking "Henry Smith" was too common. An attorney, he was a dedicated lay preacher and served as the Treasurer of Wellesley College for 11 years. His lodge is unknown, but he became a member of St. Andrew's Royal Arch Chapter of Boston on June 1, 1852.

Grand Lodge Of New England

In 2009, a legitimate-looking website, http://glsneafam.wordpress.com/, announced the Grand Lodge of Connecticut and the Grand Lodge of Rhode Island and Providence Plantations would merge to form the Grand Lodge of Southern New England on April 1 of that year. Initially generating "confusion among the craft" the posting became suspect as readers noticed the date of the merger coincided with April Fools' Day. Additionally, visitors to the site found another article detailing

the Masonic "Zombie Preparedness Plan." It didn't take long before the hoax was revealed, but in a craft of such ancient and rich traditions, this may be the best Masonic April Fools' joke ever.

William Schaw's Masonic Mark

One of the earliest examples of a Masonic mark appears on the tomb of William Schaw (1550-1602), a Scottish Freemason who was the country's Master of Works. The design forms the letters of Schaw's name overlaying a square and compasses.

The End Of The Line

Although Brother George Washington had no children, his lineage continued through his younger sibling, John Augustine Washington (1736-1787). Brother Lawrence Washington (1854-1920), John's great-great grandson and great-great grandnephew of George Washington died January 28, 1920, the last male heir in the Washington line. He was a member of Alexandria Washington Lodge 22, Alexandria, Virginia. Lawrence's death marked the end of the direct lineage of the name Washington back to the first President.

The King's Speech

With the recognition of *The King's Speech* as best motion picture of 2011, it is interesting to note that both George VI (1895-1952) and his speech therapist, Lionel George Logue (1880-1953) were Freemasons. Initiated in Naval Lodge 2612 in 1919, King George VI was an active member holding many of the highest offices in England and Scotland. WB Logue was initiated in 1908, in St George's Lodge (now JD Stevenson St. George's Lodge 6, Western Australian Constitution), where he served as Worshipful Master in 1919. King George VI said he considered Masonry to be one of the strongest influences in his life, "The world today does require spiritual and moral regeneration. I have no doubt, after many years as a member of our Order, that Freemasonry can play a most important part in this vital need."

As a matter of interest, Lodge Brothers reported of the King, "His stammer rarely surfaced when he was involved in ritual."

William McKinley

William McKinley, Eagle Lodge 431 of Canton, Ohio (Later William McKinley Lodge), was the last President of the United States who was a Civil War veteran.

The Trap Houdini Could Not Escape

With his career at its peak, world famous Harry Houdini, St. Cecile Lodge 568, New York City, always stayed at the finest hotels when he took his performances on the road. On one occasion at the ritzy Savoy Hotel in Kansas City, a guest recognized Brother Harry as he went into a phone booth to make a call. Once Houdini had closed the folding doors the guest grabbed a broom and shoved it through the door handle in a position which would prevent the doors from opening. When he finished his call, Houdini turned to find the door jammed. Although he tried everything he could, the great magician and world's most famous escape artist could not get out of the phone booth.

Hotel personnel had to rescue him and eyewitnesses reported that upon his release, Brother Houdini was quite upset and did not "subdue his passions."

Active At 95

Academy award winning actor Ernest Borgnine was a member of Abingdon Lodge 48, Abingdon, Virginia. Until his death at 95, Brother Borgnine remained an active Freemason and Honorary Chairman of the Scottish Rite RiteCare Program, which sponsors 175 Scottish Rite Childhood Language Disorders Clinics, Centers, and Programs nationwide.

The Cherry Tree Story

Mason Locke Weems (1760-1825), Lodge 50, Dumfries, Virginia, was an itinerant preacher and author. He wrote the first biography of George Washington. After several editions, Weems added a seemingly insignificant anecdote about Washington's youth. Whether that story is truth, legend or a fabrication, it unexpectedly helped the book retain its status as a best seller and needs only to be identified as, "The Cherry Tree Story." Today, it remains an icon of American folklore.

"I can not tell a lie"

The Original Quisling

Vidkun Quisling, (1887-1945) a strident Norwegian anti-Mason whose name has become synonymous with the word "traitor" collaborated with Germany in its conquest of Norway during World War II. Named head of the country by the Nazis, Quisling stripped and ruined Oslo's beautiful Masonic temple and used it for his own offices. At the end of the war he was convicted of treason and sentenced to death. In an ironic twist, his trial and sentencing took place inside a Masonic Lodge.

A Man Of Incredible Talent

Charles H. Allen, William North Lodge of Lowell, Massachusetts, became the first governor of Puerto Rico after the US freed it from Spanish rule. A man of incredible talent, he was an accomplished artist, musician and cabinet-maker. Also an avid gardener, his home, "The Terraces," boasted showcase gardens featuring fountains, a pergola, and a gazebo now located at the

University of Massachusetts Lowell, Center for Lowell History. Twenty-seven of his landscape and marine paintings are now in Lowell's Whistler House Museum of Art. As Governor of Puerto Rico, he eliminated the island's debt that had accrued over 400 years of despotic Spanish rule and incredibly left it with over a million dollars in its treasury.

An Ironic Tragedy

Brother Webster Wagner, Hamilton Lodge 79, New York, was the inventor of railroad sleeping cars. He founded the Wagner Palace-car Company, which supplied sleeping and parlor cars to all lines of the Vanderbilt system in the eastern US. Also a member of the New York state legislature, he continued to serve as his company's president until January 13, 1882, when, in an ironic tragedy, he was killed in a railroad disaster while sleeping in one of the cars he had invented.

Brother George Pullman of Renovation Lodge 97 in Albion, NY, perfected, but did not invent the railroad sleeping car, as some believe. Brother Pullman began working on his famous coaches in 1859, a year after Brother Wagner's cars first went into service.

Did You Know Grandpa Was President?

Clifton Truman Daniel, Oriental Lodge 33, Illinois, had no idea his grandfather, MWB Harry S. Truman, had been President of the United States until he started going to school, where both classmates and teachers asked him about it. "After my first day of school," he explains, "I excitedly ran home and asked my mother, 'Did you know Grandpa was

President of the United States?'" Then, with a wry smile, he will tell you, "She knew."

The King Who Rewrote The Ritual

King Charles XIII of Sweden (1748-1818), prior to taking the throne, rewrote the entire Masonic ritual used in his country. After his coronation, the King created the 11th degree of the Swedish Rite: the Civil Order of Charles XIII.

His Masonic Birthday

Self-made millionaire Sam N. Regenstrief (1909-1988), Warren Lodge 15, Connersville, Indiana, made his fortune in manufacturing and was known as the "Dishwasher King." He used his wealth to found Indianapolis' Regenstrief Institute, which developed the Regenstrief Medical Records system. Despite his wealth, philanthropy and notoriety, Brother Sam never knew his own birthdate. He was born in Bucharest, Romania and his birth records were lost. He celebrated two approximate dates as birthdays, one in June, one in November, having heard conflicting stories from relatives about the time of year he was born. He was, however, certain about one birthdate — October 28, 1948, his Masonic birthday.

Masonic Stamp Cancellations

Prior to 1895, local postmasters had the authority to make their own hand stamps for canceling postage. Not surprisingly, many incorporated the square and compasses into their personal design.

The Sands of Iwo Jima

John Wayne (1907-1979) was a member of Glendale DeMolay Chapter as a youth and became a Master Mason in Marion McDaniel Lodge 56, Tucson, Arizona in 1970. He won but a single Academy Award during his impressive acting career, for his role as the crotchety Rooster Cogburn in the 1969 film, *True Grit*. However, he also received an Oscar nomination for his portrayal of Sargent John Stryker in the 1949 classic, *The Sands of Iwo Jima*. For many years that part was considered Wayne's best work, and when Grauman's Chinese Theater honored him, the cement used to cast his footprints contained sand imported from Iwo Jima. Brother Wayne became so legendary that when Japanese Emperor Hirohito visited the United States in 1975, the only celebrity he asked to meet was John Wayne, who had become the symbolic representation of Japan's former enemy.

A Three-Time Winner

Brother Dionisio de Herrera (1781-1850), Lodge unknown, was elected president of three countries. He served as president of Honduras from 1824-27 and president of Nicaragua from 1829-34. He retired from politics and moved to El Salvador after serving his term in Nicaragua, but was so popular the people of El Salvador included him on the ballot and elected him president in 1835. Weary of politics, he declined his third presidency and turned to teaching for the remainder of his life.

Brother King?

In 1999, Most Worshipful Brother, Benjamin P. Barksdale, Grand Master of Prince Hall Freemasonry in Georgia, posthumously made Dr. Martin Luther King a Mason at sight.

The action was not without controversy, since it is one of the few instances (if not the only one) of declaring a man a Mason after his death. Dr. King's widow, Coretta Scott King, accepted the honor on behalf of her late husband. Prince Hall documentation indicates Grand Master X. L. Neal had arranged for Dr. King to become a Freemason upon his return from Atlanta in 1968, an act which was prevented by Dr. King's assassination.

Big Guy

The largest known Mason was Mills Darden (1799-1857), who weighed 1,020 pounds, stood 7'6" tall and measured 6'4" around the waist. Upon his death, it took 17 men to put him in his coffin, constructed of over 100 board-feet of lumber. His wife only weighed 90 pounds.

General Jackson's Arm

Confederate General Thomas "Stonewall" Jackson (1824-1863) lost his arm in a battle at Chancellorsville, a wound which ultimately proved fatal. Jackson's chaplain, prior to the General's death, buried the arm where it remains today, 125 miles from Jackson's grave. At that spot, he conducted a funeral for Jackson's arm and buried it with full military honors.

Based on correspondence, actions and eyewitness reports, it is likely Jackson was a Freemason, but no records exist to confirm the fact. On one occasion he was observed to return the sign of distress to a union soldier and speculation is he may have been a member of a traveling military Lodge.

Kit Carson And Mrs. White

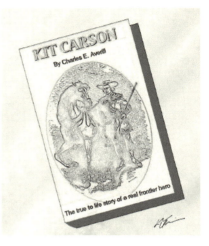

Traveling with soldiers in 1849, Christopher "Kit" Carson (1809-1868) came upon an abandoned Apache settlement. Here, Carson found the body of Ann White, who had been killed just minutes before his arrival when the Apaches had left the camp. Among her belongings, Carson found a copy of the dime novel, *Kit Carson*, by Charles Averill. The book portrayed Carson as a great hero. Carson surmised Mrs. White somehow knew he was close and might rescue her. The incident haunted Carson for the rest of his life. He spoke of it many times and wrote about it in his memoirs. Brother Kit Carson was a member of Missouri-chartered Montezuma Lodge 109 (today Montezuma Lodge 1) in Santa Fe, New Mexico.

This Ridiculous Attitude

George Washington's compressed lips in many busts and portraits are exaggerated because he tried to suppress a laugh while artist Joseph Wright was casting Washington's life mask. In Brother Washington's words, "While in this ridiculous attitude, Mrs. Washington entered the room, and seeing my face thus overspread with the plaster, involuntarily exclaimed. Her cry excited in me a disposition to smile, which gave my mouth a twist, or compression of the lips, that is now observable in the busts Wright afterward made."

Mason City, Iowa

Is Mason City, Iowa named after the Freemasons? Yes... and no... Brother John Long originally named Iowa prairie land along the Winnebago River Masonic Grove in honor of the Freemasons. Later, Long, Joseph Hewitt and George Brentner renamed it Shibboleth, a name also familiar to Freemasons. Then, when bringing his family to the area from Illinois, Long's son, Mason, died. Upon returning to the town, he renamed it Masonville, in honor of his son. In 1853, however, while erecting the post office there, the city fathers discovered there were two towns in Iowa with that name, so they renamed it Mason City, the name it carries today. After incorporation in 1870, Darius Mason became the first mayor. In the early 1950s, the real Mason City became the fictional River City when Meredith Willson's *Music Man* had its debut. Today Mason City, Willson's home town, hosts the annual Mason City Band Festival in tribute its rich cultural history.

Historic Meeting

On May 5, 2011, the Brothers of Polar Star Rose Hill Lodge 79 in Creve Coeur, Missouri, United States and the Brothers of Salomon à trois Serrures Lodge in Göteborg, Sweden jointly opened their Lodges on the Third Degree of Freemasonry. The historic meeting was the first Masonic meeting ever to be held by two Lodges on different continents. During the special communication over live video facilitated by Internet technology, the Brothers discussed the customs, ritual and activities of each Lodge. The Grand Lodges of both jurisdictions sanctioned the event.

Aided By His Own Fund

Anthony Sayer (1672-1742), England's first Grand Master, 1717-18, established a Grand Lodge charity fund. Upon leaving office, Brother Sayer fell on hard times and became the first person to receive financial assistance from that fund.

Five Stars

Brother Gene Autry was more of a superstar than most realize. In fact, of all celebrities past and present, Brother Autry is the only one to have five stars on the Hollywood Walk of Fame: for radio, recording, motion pictures, television and live theater/performance.

The Grand Hailing Sign of Distress

In contrast to the grueling 12-day siege at the Alamo, the Texans routed the Mexican army at San Jacinto in a mere 18 minutes. In the process, they also captured General Santa Anna. It is a puzzle to some historians as to why the Texans did not summarily execute Santa Anna, who had shown no mercy at the Alamo. Some, including Masonic historian William R. Denslow are certain there is only one reasonable explanation why the Texans spared Santa Anna. He was, in fact, Brother Antonio López de Santa Anna, a Freemason. Reports exist that General Santa Anna not once, but three times, gave the Grand Hailing Sign of Distress including making the gesture personally to Brother Sam Houston himself. Together, Houston and

other Brothers who had witnessed this granted their Brother Santa Anna the Masonic compassion he had denied others at the Alamo.

Oldest Known Masonic Monument

The United States' oldest known Masonic monument was placed on the Boston Road outside Springfield, Massachusetts. A Masonic soldier, Colonel Wait, erected it at the spot where he was lost in a snowstorm, as a testimony to God for saving his life.

The Mysterious Number 33

The mysterious number "33" appearing on the back of Rolling Rock beer cans and bottles has led to speculation that, among other theories, it refers to the 33rd degree of the Scottish Rite. The company has explained it as a printer's error. A company executive had written the number at the end of the text referring to the number of words in the blurb. The printer thought it was meant to be there and included it. Rather than remove the number, the company left it there and has gotten a lot of mileage out of the speculation surrounding it.

A Familiar Name

In 1953, the Grand Chaplain of the Grand Lodge of Texas was a Brother named Hiram Abiff Boaz.

Honorable To His Memory

Abraham Lincoln expressed a desire to become a Freemason prior to becoming a candidate for the presidency, and even made application to his hometown Lodge. However, once a candidate, he thought his effort to join would be construed to be a political move. Instead, He advised the Lodge he would resubmit his application when he returned from the presidency. On April 17, 1865 with the nation still reeling from the news of Lincoln's death, Tyrian Lodge 333 of Springfield, Illinois passed the following resolution: "The first thought of a Mason should be, as his duty is, to trust in God. Resolved, that the decision of President Lincoln to postpone his application for the honors of Masonry, lest his motives should be misconstrued, is in the highest degree honorable to his memory."

The Lodge That Was Open For 50 Years

Hiram Lodge 40, Raleigh North Carolina, was in session when news of President Lincoln's assassination arrived. Presiding Master John Nichols did not wait to close the Lodge as Brothers rushed to return to their homes. The Lodge remained open for 50 years. In a special ceremony on the 50th anniversary of the opening, April 17, 1915, WB John Nichols himself presided over the official closing.

Unmasonic Conduct

Worshipful Brother Sam Houston (1793-1863), was an American patriot, congressman, US Senator, governor of Tennessee, hero of the Texas fight for independence, president of the Republic of Texas, governor of Texas, Past Master, member of several Lodges, Royal Arch Mason and more. Yet, in 1828, one of his Lodges suspended him for unmasonic conduct.

The proceedings list no reason for Brother Houston's suspension, but it may relate to an earlier dueling incident or, being Governor of Tennessee at the time, it may have been a political matter. Whatever the case, he was reinstated and remained a "true and faithful Brother among us" for the remainder of his life.

Anti-Masonic Impeachment

It's a well-known fact Brother Andrew Johnson, Greeneville Lodge 119, Greeneville, Tennessee, is one of only two presidents to be impeached. Lesser known is the fact that Johnson's main antagonist in the impeachment was vehement anti-Mason Thaddeus Stevens. Johnson's dedication to the Craft played a significant role in prompting Stevens to take action against him.

The Illumination

John Fitzgerald Kennedy participated in a Masonic ceremony on October 6, 1962. While flying over the area, JFK pushed a button which, by remote control illuminated a statue the Grand Lodge of Illinois was rededicating. The statue in downtown Chicago honored Brothers George Washington, Robert Morris and Haym Solomon.

First

Shadrach Bond (1773-1832) was not only the first Grand Master of Illinois, but also was the state's first Governor.

He Funded A War

John Jacob Astor, (1763-1848) one of the richest men of his time, was one of the first members of Holland Lodge 8, New York City, and served as its Master in 1788. He was also the Grand Treasurer of the Grand Lodge of New York from 1798-1801. Brother Astor was so wealthy he partially funded the War of 1812 by making huge loans to the US Government.

Hate Stamps

Following the Nazi occupation in 1941, Serbia issued a series of anti-Masonic, anti-Jewish stamps to promote the Grand Anti-Masonic Exhibition, which opened in Belgrade October 22, 1941. Each of the four stamps depicts a victorious Serbia defeating plots for world domination.

First Trans-Pacific Flight

Brother Charles Lindbergh's first flight across the Atlantic in 1927 made him world famous. Lesser known, however is the flight of Brothers Lester J. Maitland and Albert F. Hegenberger just a few weeks later. Together, they completed the first trans-Pacific flight from California to Hawaii in what is seen as a greater navigational feat. Although Lindbergh garnered all the notoriety (and, along with it, tragedy) Maitland, a member of Kenwood Lodge 303 in Milwaukee, went on to a successful military and aeronautics career and eventually became an Episcopal minister. Hegenberger, a Mason, Knight Templar and Shriner, was an attorney who went on to a political career serving as Mayor of Oklahoma City from 1939-1947.

Born In A Teepee

Brother Parker Paul McKenzie (1897-1999) was a Kiowa Native American. Born in a teepee, he was educated at the Rainy Mountain Kiowa Boarding school where the Kiowa language was banned and anyone using it was subject to harsh punishment. As an adult, Brother McKenzie vowed to preserve the language which, up to that time was strictly oral. He developed the Kiowa alphabet, documented its vocabulary and translated several works into the language. Without a formal higher-education, the University of Colorado awarded him an honorary doctorate and at his death he was the oldest living Kiowa.

Five Days

Brother Milton Latham, Washington Lodge 20 of Sacramento, had the shortest term of any California Governor, serving only five days.

First To Display The Flag

Cosmos Lodge 282 claims to be the first Masonic Lodge west of the Mississippi regularly to display the American Flag at meetings. In 1896, it began displaying this 44-star flag, when former Missouri Grand Master John D. Vincil (1868-1869) presented it to the Lodge. The flag is on display at the Masonic Museum in Columbia, Missouri.

Wrong Place At The Wrong Time

John R. Thomas (1846-1914), Grand Master of the Grand Lodge of Illinois (1885), moved to Oklahoma to practice law after serving 10 years in congress. In a classic case of being in the wrong place at the wrong time, on January 20, 1914, MWB Thomas elected to meet with a client in the warden's office of the Oklahoma state prison in McAlester to discuss a case. At the same moment, three convicts who had obtained a gun made an escape attempt, but first headed for the warden's office to confront a parole officer. Brother Thomas was the first to die in the botched plot that ultimately saw the three convicts, the deputy warden and two other prison officials killed.

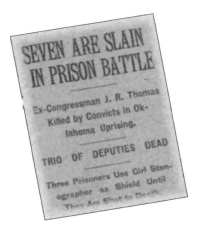

Club 33

Although many people have speculated about Walt Disney's Masonic ties, he was not a Freemason. However, Disney was in fact a DeMolay and was always supportive of the Masonic fraternity. He even sponsored a Magic Kingdom Mason's club for the employees in his parks. He also created the very exclusive Club 33 on his Magic Kingdom  campus which caused further speculation about his Masonic status. Membership in the lavish Club 33 is quite expensive. Although some members are known (mainly corporate memberships), the roster is supposed to be "secret," which further fuels the crazed conspiracy theorist frenzy. In 2012, Disney Corporation announced it would open membership to the mysterious club for the first time in a decade. Reports say only 13 new spots were open. Those lucky enough to get one could expect to pay a $25,000 initiation fee and annual dues of $10,000. A spot on the waiting list is free but, unfortunately the waiting list is full, too. It's also a secret who's on the waiting list and should you get on it, your position on the list is secret, even to you. It must be Masonic.

Devastating Day

In what was certainly the most devastating day of his life, Theodore Roosevelt's mother and wife both died on the same day, February 14, 1884, Valentine's day — and also the 4th anniversary of his wedding. The entry in his diary for that day contained a single sentence, "The light has gone out of my life."

The double tragedy so crushed the 25-year old future president that he quit politics and left New York, moving to the "Badlands" in the Dakota territories.

Frank E. Hering

Frank E. Hering (1874-1943), South Bend Lodge 294, Indiana, was the first Notre Dame basketball coach and also coached its football team. He expanded the football program from a small intramural activity to a full-fledged intercollegiate competition. He also served as President of the Fraternal Order of Eagles form 1909-12, and used  that forum to promote the establishment of a national Mother's Day. Successful in all these endeavors, he is known both as "The Father of Notre Dame Football" and "The Father of Mother's Day."

By The Grace Of God And Two Revolvers

John M. Chivington (1821-1894) was the first Master of the first Lodge in Kansas and also the first Grand Master of Colorado. A Methodist minister, Brother Chivington was paradoxically both a missionary to Native American tribes and an Indian fighter. He was such a staunch abolitionist his predominately pro-slavery Missouri congregation threatened to tar and feather  him. His reaction was to take the pulpit with a Bible and two pistols and announce, "By the grace of God and these two revolvers, I am going to preach here today."

Brother Chivington was a controversial figure after commanding the ruthless Indian massacre at Sand Creek. In his later years however, he softened and returned to the values of his church and

Freemasonry. When he died in October of 1894, more than 500 Brethren attended his funeral.

The Iowa Corn Song

Des Moines Brother George E. Hamilton wrote Iowa's "unofficial" state song, the *Iowa Corn Song*, for Za-Ga-Zig Shriners to sing at a Shriner's convention in Los Angeles in 1912. The song became extremely popular, with other composers chiming in with their own verses. Brother Hamilton didn't copyright it, not realizing he had written a runaway hit.

His Final Signature

Warren G. Harding, a member of Marion Lodge 70, Marion, Ohio, was the 29th President of the United States. He died in office August 2, 1923. In failing health, he visited Lafayette Lodge 241 in Seattle just days before his death. He canceled all appearances after that, making the Lodge visit his final public function, and the final time Brother Harding signed his name was in the Lodge's Bible.

The American Legion

In 1918 a group of twenty officers met in France to suggest ideas on how to improve troop Morale. Theodore Roosevelt, Jr., son of the former President, proposed forming an organization of veterans to support the troops and provide them with a source of continued fellowship after their military service was over. That suggestion led to the formation of the American Legion, which congress formally chartered the following year. Brother Roosevelt, a member of his father's Lodge, Matinecock Lodge 806 of Oyster Bay, New York, went on to become a World War II hero, winning the Congressional Medal of Honor shortly before his death in 1944.

The Chief Justice Who Wasn't

Every school kid learns John Jay, whose Masonic status is uncertain, was the first Chief Justice of the US Supreme Court. But most do not know the first Associate Justice was William Cushing (1732-1810), a member of St. Andrew's Lodge, Boston. Brother Cushing had been Attorney General of Massachusetts and became the state's first Chief Justice in 1772. Cushing, in fact, was the first person Brother Washington appointed to the Supreme Court, even before appointing Jay. In 1796, Washington appointed Cushing the 3rd Chief Justice. The Senate unanimously confirmed Cushing and that evening he attended a dinner party where Washington surprised him by praising his virtues and asking him to sit on his right had side. Cushing, in return, surprised Washington when, a few days later, he declined the appointment.

Apparently, health and family matters were the reasons why Cushing declined, although he did continue to serve as Associate justice until his death in 1810. Of the original Supreme Court Justices, Brother Cushing served the longest, 21 years.

Masonic Baptism

In the late 19th and early 20th centuries, many Lodges in the United States and Europe conducted Masonic baptisms. During the ceremony, written by Albert Pike, the presiding officer gave the child Masonic emblems, promising him or her the protection of the fraternity. While the ritual for the ceremony survives, it is rarely performed today.

American Gothic

Brother Grant Wood (1892-1942), of Mount Hermon Lodge 263, Cedar Rapids, painted the acclaimed "American Gothic." Released in 1930 the painting caused a scandal when Wood said it was a married couple, due to their apparent age difference. Wood eventually said the woman represented the man's daughter, but would change that story and say she was his wife, depending on how he perceived the audience would react.

Masonic Weddings

Weddings in Lodges are not very common, but they do take place now and then. They were more common in the past and today are more prevalent in Europe than in the US. French Lodges frequently have a "conjugal recognition" ceremony, which is not actually a wedding. In Turkey, Lodges have a book-length official Masonic wedding ceremony. In the US, weddings are held in Masonic Lodges with varying degrees of Masonic connection. Some Lodges with facilities to accommodate crowds only serve as the venue, in many cases with couples who have no connections to the Craft. Other times, however, Brothers will elect to marry in the Lodge and attribute more significance to taking their vows in the Lodge room itself.

Winston Churchill's Birth

An urban legend has floated around the Internet for years claiming Brother Winston Churchill was born in a ladies' room at a dance. It isn't true, but hearing the circumstances of his birth, one can see how the rumor got started. Churchill's mother, Jennie, was attending a dance at Blenheim Palace when she went into labor. She was removed to a "singularly bleak-looking bedroom" which was temporarily being used to store coats (hence, folklore seems to have translated "cloakroom," into "ladies' room"). There, 24 hours after the dance had ended, Winston was born.

Andrew Jackson Decapitated!

In 1834, the venerable USS Constitution, launched in 1797, the most celebrated vessel of the War of 1812, was destined for the scrap heap. Heeding a public outcry, Brother Andrew Jackson, then president, stepped in and saved the iconic ship. In gratitude the group charged with restoring the Constitution replaced its figurehead with a likeness of Jackson. The gesture infuriated Jackson's enemies who, three months later, sneaked aboard and decapitated the statue. The following year, a new head replaced the old one and that figurehead remained in place for fifteen years until a new statue of Jackson in a Napoleonic pose replaced it. The severed head resurfaced as a conversation piece in the taverns of New York until it was eventually returned to Mahlon Dickerson, Secretary of the Navy, but with the lower part containing the mouth missing. It was not until 2010 that the two pieces were reunited, when a Public Broadcasting crew rediscovered the missing lower section.

The Versatile Arthur Conan Doyle

Sir Arthur Conan Doyle (1859-1930), best known as the Author of the Sherlock Holmes Series, was raised in Phoenix Lodge 257, Hampshire. In addition to writing the books about the famous sleuth, Doyle was a physician, author of many books and short stories on other subjects, a spiritualist and a sportsman. He was an early proponent of a tunnel connecting England and France, metal helmets for combat soldiers, and inflatable life-preservers for sailors. In 1894, on a US visit, he introduced Rudyard Kipling to golf, with confused locals wondering what the pair was up to as they played; and amazingly, he also introduced cross country skiing to the Swiss.

A Wonderful But Terrifying Discovery

Brother Arthur Sullivan was a noted 19th century composer (of Gilbert & Sullivan fame), author of *Onward Christian Soldiers*, and Grand Organist of the Grand Lodge of England. Upon hearing his music played on one of the earliest recordings, the amazed Sullivan told Thomas Edison, "I can only say that I am astonished and somewhat terrified at the result of this evening's experiments: astonished at the wonderful power you have developed, and terrified at the thought that so much hideous and bad music may be put on record forever. But all the same I think it is the most wonderful thing that I have ever experienced, and I congratulate you with all my heart on this wonderful discovery."

An Eternal Honor

Joseph G. Cannon (1836-1926), Olive Branch Lodge 38 of Danville, was an Illinois congressman who served as Speaker of the US House of Representatives most years from 1903-11. Time magazine's report on his retirement earned him the eternal honor of having his picture on its first cover, March 3, 1923.

No Fighting

A resolution in Massachusetts' Bristol Lodge, founded in 1797, read as follows: "No liquor shall be brought into the Lodge except by order of the Master. Fighting is forbidden during the opening or within 30 minutes of the closing of the Lodge.

The Only Korean Cornerstone

There are four Masonic Lodges in the Republic of Korea: Han Yang Lodge 1048, Lodge Pusan 1675, and Lodge Harry S. Truman 1727, each chartered under the Grand Lodge of Scotland. MacArthur

Lodge 183 holds its charter from the Grand Lodge of the Philippines. The only known Masonic cornerstone in the country is at the Pusan (Busan) Children's Charity Hospital. Masonic members of the US Armed forces, the hospital's sponsor, placed the cornerstone in 1955.

Like Father Like Son

Arthur MacArthur, Jr., Magnolia Lodge 60, Little Rock, known as "The Boy Colonel," was a hero of the Civil War honored for "seizing colors of his regiment at critical moment and planting them on the captured works on the crest of Missionary Ridge in 1863." He and his son, Brother Douglas MacArthur (Manila Lodge 1, Philippines,), General of the Army in WWII, are the only father and son recipients of the Congressional Medal of Honor.

Temperate Temperance

Mark Twain and temperance zealot Carrie Nation reportedly met only once, when Ms. Nation attacked a saloon Twain was patronizing one evening. Sketchy details about the incident indicate her tirade irritated Brother Twain, who confronted her, prior to her arrest. Mark Twain (a.k.a. Samuel Clemens) described himself as being an advocate of "temperate temperance."

17 Lodges On Three Continents

Canon William Henry Cooper founded St. Luke's Hospital for the Clergy, London, in 1892 and died there in 1909. Brother Cooper was a member of no less than 17 Lodges on three continents, including Lodges in Ireland, England, Australia, New Zealand, British Columbia and Ontario. He was also the founder and first Master of three of his Lodges.

Don't Shoot — We're Republicans

Brother Franklin D. Roosevelt, Holland Lodge 8 of New York City, crossed the Atlantic in November 1943, to attend a World War II summit. While the President was en-route traveling on the *USS Iowa* battleship, the navy arranged a demonstration of firepower for its commander-in-chief. At the start of the trip the battleship *William D. Porter* joined the *Iowa* to show off its capabilities for FDR. During the demonstration, crew members inadvertently fired a live torpedo at the President's ship. Learning this, Brother Roosevelt asked to be taken deck-side so he could watch! Forced to take evasive action, the *Iowa* barely avoided the live "fish." Roosevelt, a Democrat, took the incident in stride, but from that time on, whenever the "*Willie D*" pulled into port crew members from other ships would yell in ridicule, "Don't shoot — we're Republicans!"

Hey, Look Him Over

In the 1962 Indiana Senatorial campaign, young Democratic upstart Birch Bayh went up against the venerable Republican incumbent Homer E. Capehart, in a relatively conservative state where young Bayh's chances were not seen as very good. The two candidates, Masonic Brothers, went after each other in a brutal campaign that was too close to predict right down to the bitter end. Toward the end of the race, Bayh's campaign staff came up with  new words to a little ditty from a 1960 Broadway show starring Lucille Ball, *Wildcat*. The song was *Hey, Look Me Over*. The catchy song was so successful analysts said it was a significant factor in Brother Bayh's astonishing upset victory. Six years later, when Bayh was up for re-election, Republicans took no chances. They purchased the rights to the song and put it on the shelf. Brother Birch Bayh won anyway, and went on to a stellar career in the US Senate. Briefly, in 1976, he was considered a front-runner for the Democratic Presidential nomination.

A Frivolous Tune

 Forrest Adair, Past Potentate of Yaarab Temple, Atlanta, was an attendee at the June, 1920, Imperial Session in Portland, Oregon, which was considering the establishment of a Shrine Hospital for Children. Delegates had suggested funding the hospital with a $2 assessment to each member, but support for the project was unenthusiastic. Brother Adair was somewhat resigned to the fact that the delegates would scrub the proposal.

Early on the morning of the vote, however, a minstrel, possibly inebriated, stood beneath his hotel room window playing *I'm Forever*

Blowing Bubbles on his horn. The song, about wasting time with frivolity, woke Adair and its meaning stuck with him. He related it to the activities of the Shrine which, although it had its various charities at the time, was more about having fun.

That afternoon at the session, as the delegates wrangled and the idea of a hospital seemed lost, Brother Adair arose and spoke passionately about his experience early that morning, "I am reminded of that wandering minstrel, and I wonder if there is not a deep significance for the Shriners in the tune that he was playing, *I'm Forever Blowing Bubbles*. While we have spent money for songs and spent money for bands, it's time for the Shrine to spend money for humanity. I want to see this thing started. Let's get rid of all the technical objections. And if there is a Shriner in North America who objects to having paid the two dollars after he has seen the first crippled child helped, I will give him a check back for it myself." After Adair's speech, not only did the resolution pass unanimously but it also spawned a committee whose research indicated the Shrine should build not one, but a nationwide network of Hospitals.

Oak Island

A mysterious pit on Oak Island in Nova Scotia has led many to believe it is the site of a great buried treasure. Long thought to be pirate bounty, the discovery of Masonic signs, symbols and working tools there lead many researchers to believe the site is of Masonic origin. Characteristics of the pit itself closely  parallel Masonic degree symbology. Some researchers believe the Holy Grail or Arc of the Covenant may be buried there, while skeptics believe the site may even be a hoax. Oak Island is so captivating Freemasons Robert Byrd, John Wayne and even Franklin Roosevelt have journeyed to the obscure island to search for themselves. The frustrating effort to get to whatever is buried there continues today after over two centuries of digging.

Impostors

A fraternity that performs so many charitable acts is bound to be the target of fraud. Those impersonating Masons for financial gain and those appealing to Masonic charities under false pretenses have been around almost as long as the order itself. Today, with the Internet and mass media, word can spread quickly when a charlatan surfaces. In times past, such communication was slower and more difficult.
In 1859, Rob Morris, founder of the Eastern Star, published *The Prudence Book*. Updated annually, it was an attempt to publish information about impostors, but was discontinued after a short run. It was found easier to print and distribute "broadsides" as Lodges discovered impostors.

The Reunion

The Marquis de La Fayette, a champion of human rights, worked with the slave Armistad in the American Revolution to infiltrate Cornwallis' camp and together they outsmarted and defeated the general. Lafayette and Armistad became such good friends that upon gaining his freedom, Armistad changed his name to James Armistead Lafayette. After the revolution, Lafayette went back to France, but returned years later for the 50th anniversary celebration of United States independence. His return was a triumphant tour of the country during which the state of Virginia held an enormous parade in his honor. Along the parade route Lafayette recognized his old friend

Armistad in the crowd and surprised the spectators when he stopped the procession and went to greet him. The two men had a tearful but joyful reunion. While on the tour, Lafayette, a man of many Masonic Honors, became an honorary member of the Grand Lodge of Missouri.

The Freemason

The 2013 movie, *The Freemason*, was filmed at the venerable Salt Lake City Masonic Temple. It won "Filmed In Utah" awards for Best Actor (Sean Astin) and Best Supporting Actor (Richard Dutcher). The film's producer, Joseph James, is a member of multiple Lodges in several states as well as the Shrine, Scottish Rite and York Rite. Brother James has produced three films, all dealing with Freemasonry.

Inverted

An inverted square and compasses marks Brother William T. Reynolds grave in Liberty, Missouri. The inscription on the tombstone reads, "Mar. 13, 1826 Died in Liberty, Mo. by the hands of an assassin." The inverted square and compasses, among other things, signifies distress.

Debts Owed

Missouri Lodge 12, Joachim Lodge 25 and St. Charles Lodge 28 met in 1821 to form the Grand Lodge of Missouri. The Grand Lodge of Tennessee held the charters to all three Lodges, and upon learning of the formation of the Missouri Grand Lodge, withheld recognition as a result of the debts owed by the three Lodges. The total amount owed was only $17 (approximately $300 in today's funds). The Missouri Lodges ignored Tennessee's action and the Grand Lodge of Missouri was born. Both Grand Lodges report that in the ensuing years they have amicably settled their differences.

Purple Heart

Brother George Washington instituted the Purple Heart (Badge of Military Merit) as the first award to go to the common soldier. After the American Revolution, the Purple Heart was not awarded for 149 years when, on May 28, 1932, 138 World War I veterans retroactively received their Purple Hearts.

And Finally...

I mentioned in the preface that *Did You Know*, compiled from a collection of vignettes which originally appeared in the *Royal Arch Magazine*, provided the inspiration for this book. I re-researched many of those stories and included them here; but most of the items in this book came from elsewhere. When I started the project I figured after I ran out of *Did You Know* stories, others would be hard to find.

They weren't. Freemasons and their fraternity are interesting. I suppose you could extend that to everyone. Each of us has probably had something happen that was fascinating, quirky, a story with a twist or we may have done something really significant that would have made a good story in this book. I know I have. I didn't include any stories about myself, but I included a few about people I knew. I could have included accounts of my three encounters with "flying saucers," even though I am a confirmed skeptic on that subject; or, there was the time I started a measles epidemic. You can read about those things on the *Midnight Freemasons* blog. The point is I've got my stories, too. We all do. What are yours?

About the Author

Steven L. Harrison, 33°, FMLR, is Past Master of Liberty Lodge 31, Liberty, Missouri and is a dual member of Kearney Lodge 311. His other Masonic affiliations include Liberty York Rite Bodies, Scottish Rite Valley of St. Joseph and Moila Shrine. As a youth, he was a member of Oriental Chapter, Order of DeMolay in Indianapolis, where he received the Chevalier award and served as Master Councilor. In 2009, he was awarded the DeMolay Legion of Honor and is Past Dean of its St. Joseph Preceptory. Steve was named a Fellow of the Missouri Lodge of Research (FMLR) in 2011 and served as its Master in 2013-14. He is a regular contributor to the *Midnight Freemasons* blog, *The Working Tools Magazine* and other Masonic publications. He has been editor of the *Missouri Freemason* magazine since 2005. With a Master's degree from Indiana University Bloomington, he is retired from a 35-year career in information technology. Steve and his wife Carolyn reside in Kearney, Missouri.